MAKE BANK 2022

The Best Guide for Turning Your Finance Using Proven and Profitable Strategies

Disclaimer

Here's the disclaimer my lawyers want everyone to accept and agree to. But I'm going to write it in my words, not theirs:

It is possible for you to lose all of your money emulating what I do here. That's because there are exceptions to every rule. There are black swans and unpredictable events. If any investment strategy was guaranteed, then it wouldn't be an investment. And that includes your safe job, which you can lose at any moment. All the more reason I want to share these strategies with you.

What worked and continues to work for me may not work for you. Hell, it may not continue to work for me. Is an asteroid headed this way? I have no idea.

I'm not making any of this up. It isn't voodoo. It's my journey down the rabbit hole of creative banking and how I've found financial freedom because of it.

Proceed with caution, but also an open-mind and a healthy dose of optimism.

CONTENTS

1
Think Like A Bank

2
How To Become A Loan Shark

3
Profit From Peer Pressure

4
Stabilize Income With A Coin

5
Give Leverage To Speculators

6
Let Wall Street Pay You

7
Collect Mortgage Payments

8
Don't Buy Your House

9
Trust Delaware For Wealth

10
Multiply Money With Multi-families

11
Present Value Of Future Money

12
No-brainer Extra Income

13
Bank Yourself For Infinite Value

1

Think Like A Bank

"Bankers are just like anyone else, only richer."

- Ogden Nash

I never have to "work" again if I don't want to. That guy you see on the front cover with the pipe of cash flowing out isn't hyperbole. That's me. Of course, I don't have the chiseled jaw with the 25 inch biceps. I also don't own a tie. But other than that, I have a system where money pours into my accounts because I've opened the money valve to transform my finances.

I put "work" in quotes because I honestly love what I do. So I don't consider it work. And one of the things I do is help others get what they want. In this case, that's money. Because I know everyone wants money.

I know people make fun of bankers. Like accountants, they're an easy target. We portray them as boring, stiff, and unimaginative. Part of that may be true because they don't have to be too creative to make piles of money. They simply have to know where the opportunity is. And then essentially do one thing: they lend.

It couldn't be simpler than that.

This banking business model has been around since the dawn of history. The Qur'an and Christian Bible have vilified and banned lending if it involved collecting interest. Jews were also persecuted for attempting to lend. The Torah implies that Jews can only lend to strangers. It says they can only give (not lend) money to other Jews, friends or family members, and expect nothing in return.

In Italy and other countries, Jews weren't allowed to own land and grow wealth like everyone else. So they began lending out money to *strangers* to make money. They conducted their business outside in courtyards while sitting on... *banques*. Eventually Italy wanted in on the action and formed the worlds' first merchant bancas, or "banks."

Banks are the supreme leaders in the lending space. But they don't just give you a small business loan for your new mobile hamster pedicure business. They involve themselves in activities and products, most effectively risk-free, that until recently no one knew about or had access to.

All that has evolved is that it's now easier than ever to lend and borrow because of technology. We don't have to sit on benches that sound like banks to give someone money that sounds like a loan.

Outside of Wall Street bankers, the other 99% aren't aware of the opportunity. Without the tools of the banker, one wouldn't know where to look or begin.

Main Street is sold a story about working hard, paying bills, and then putting 10% away in a savings account for a rainy day. Mom and pop relinquish control and let an institution invest for them. But those brokers and investment bankers are making the lion's share, not mom and pop.

There are alternative investments you may have never heard of. If you only have $25 to your name, that's enough to start the Bank of You. And If you have that with three or four zeros tacked on, you'll dive into the adult pool where the fat whales bask. Regardless where you are on your investing journey, these concepts will help you navigate the financial waters.

If you're an expert in investment concepts and grasp blended rates, LTV, ARV, RTV, DTI ratios, capital stacks, net present value, syndicates, depreciation taxes, arbitrage, DeFi, etc., you've got a running start.

For everyone else, I'm removing the academic barriers and detouring onto Easy Street. We just want to make money that was once reserved for the 1%.

Banks want you to enjoy the experience of banking with them. They offer free accounts, personalize-your-own debit cards, tempting cash sign-up bonuses, no fee offers, 0% credit swaps, and free lobby coffee.

But none of that makes you money. It's just wrapping paper covering a present whose only surprise is that you aren't making money. And nobody really wants the bank's coffee. I'd rather bank at Starbucks than get coffee at a bank.

Your money is always safe with a bank. That's the ethos. You identity with their logo. You get support, friendly greetings, and short wait times. You feel a sense of community (as in rooting for your favorite sports team, but without the over-priced beer and annoying foam finger poking you in the back every 7 minutes).

The truth? The minute you deposit money with a bank, they turn around and leverage it in the form of mortgages, business loans, securities, lines of credit, credit card advances, and other arbitrage opportunities. They often make an unimaginable 20%+ on the spread of various strategies from your near 0% savings account.

Even if you own stocks, they are being loaned out to others by your brokerage bank. It's called SEC Lending, and it's one of the biggest bank secrets. They are making money lending out your stocks to traders at 15% interest rates. And they don't share those profits with you. In fact you have to get out a magnifying glass and dig into the 5pt fonts to see that the SEC makes this completely legal.

The classic bank robbery movies we view are fairy tales. Almost no bank today has an actual iron vault with stacks and stacks of cash and gold bars. They know better than we that if it's sitting there it's not making money. So 90% of it - 90% of *your* money - is out of their hands making *them* money.

And, as difficult as it is to fathom, during the COVID-19 pandemic, banks were allowed to lend out all of your money - every penny. As of March 26, 2020, the board of the Federal Reserve required 0% of depositor's funds to be on hand with banks.

This is completely legal, fractional banking. The bank is estimating - essentially betting - not every customer will wake up one day and withdraw their money. That would be a nightmare. It's similar to the mentality of airlines overbooking and hoping some decide not to fly that day.

When there are bank-runs in countries like Venezuela, Cypress, Brazil, or Zimbabwe, banks have to shut down or limit daily withdrawals to pocket change. But it's all perfectly legal. It's a legal Ponzi scheme encouraged by world governments. It's how politicians control the money supply and thus inflate and deflate the economy.

The more the Fed insists banks lend out, the more money that is pumped into the economy. It props up the marketplace. Consumers can get cheap loans, start businesses, invest in stock markets, and pay employees. Everyone is happy. Everyone consumes.

That is, until inflation sets in. When this much money is eased into the economy, prices naturally rise to accommodate the demand. And savings rates plummet. Though you think you're gaining, you're not; inflation is beating you.

The converse is also true. When times are so irresponsibly good and getting frothy, we start to see expanding bubbles. The government prophylactically restricts what banks can lend by raising rates. Savers retreat to a bank's safety with higher interest rates. Why risk a volatile, over-inflated stock market when you can make similar interest in a bank? That's the theory. That's the story banks tell. But it's a lie.

When you deposit money at a bank, you are just handing your leverage and sovereignty over to them. Behavioral economists and cognitive psychologists will tell you we accept this lie because of loss aversion. We are wired to prefer not losing a certain amount over gaining the same amount.

Let me illustrate.

You're in Vegas gambling at a table by yourself. You've just spent 2 hours working your way up to a $300 profit at the blackjack table. You are excited and ready to stop when suddenly your friends sidle up to the felt with drinks and drunk smiles, and beg you to stay and play with them. You begrudgingly continue, only to now lose the $300 you just won.

As you all walk away from the gin-and-tonic soaked floors, the rest of the night's mood is now tarnished with your $300 loss. You had that $300 gain right before your friends showed up, but then gave it all back. What a bummer.

Roll Sound. Camera's up. Take 2:

You're gambling for 2 hours by yourself and you lose $300. Damn, you're in the hole! Your friends sidle up to the table with those same strong drinks and Vegas-Baby smiles. They beg you to join them. You reluctantly dig in and keep playing to socialize, even though you're down $300.

After 2 hours playing with your friends you've managed to now win your $300 back!

The rest of the night is amazing as your heroic story permeates the overly air-conditioned ventilation. You won your money back. What a great feeling.

Both scenes are identical. You ended up even in each take.

But this heuristic highlights why as investors we are happy keeping our money "safe" even though it's not making anything. We'd rather not lose $100 than potentially make $100. And that's why we accept .01% interest rates at our retail banks.

You can have your cake and eat it too by being your own bank. And you probably won't serve the overheated Mr. Coffee with complimentary powdered creamer.

People need dependable income. That can come from unlimited sources when you think like a bank. Although these aren't passive enough for my taste, you can earn money with creative lending; like:

- leasing out your car on Turo

- renting out your parking space on CurbFlip

- leasing out extra storage space in your house on NeighborStorage

- renting out your bike or surfboard on Spinlister

- renting your clothes on StyleLend

- sharing an extra room in your house on AirBnb

You can lend out practically anything you own from prom and wedding dresses to garden tools. In a way, those are all bank-like.

Our connected economy allows access and monetization for all of this. The power has shifted to those who lend because no one wants to own anymore. It's too expensive. Renting and borrowing makes more sense.

But physically renting out your foldable ladder or your star-gazer 3000 telescope requires too much time and hassle. It's not automated or passive.

If you have spare time and energy, this concept may work for you. I've been there. But I have much more effective and profitable methods now that I understand the approach and process of an investment banker.

Again, I like to simply turn on that money valve and let it come gushing out.

I have long-term investing strategies. You should, too. Retirement plans, mutual funds, and compounding interest make a lot of sense. There's no disputing that. They're simply not the focus of this book.

This book is about the here-and-now more than the there-and-tomorrow. Tomorrow may happen. But let's make *now* profitable by adopting the banker's mindset.

Here's what I will share with you in the upcoming chapters:

You can connect to borrowers from anywhere in the country and lend to them for as little as $25 with the click of a mouse. You'll make at least 400x more than the bank currently pays you (chapter 3).

You can drop into the Matrix to lend to Bitcoiners for guaranteed interest rates of over 8.6%, whether or not you care about Bitcoin. You'll make over 800x what your retail savings account pays (chapters 4 and 5).

You can lend to Wall Street for tax-advantaged monthly income no matter if the stock market is up or down. Your earning potential is almost unlimited (chapter 6).

You can own the mortgages of builders, developers, and flippers; and have their properties as legal collateral. You'll make over 1,000x what the bank pays you (chapter 7).

You can buy dirt-cheap out-of-state income properties because they're 1/40th the cost in your state, and earn 5x the rate of rent (chapter 8).

You can then convert those same cheap income properties into a trust where you'll earn virtually unlimited tax-free income forever, never paying any capital gains tax (chapter 9).

You can club with others like me in large apartment complexes to earn over 20% a year without dealing with toilets, trash, or tenants (chapter 10).

You can earn high interest rates from alternative instruments like lawsuit settlements or popular artwork (chapter 11).

You can reduce unnecessary expenses you didn't realize you had in order to have more money you didn't even know was possible. (chapter 12).

And in the end, you can share your knowledge, lending out your time to help accelerate the journey of others, which compounds yours (chapter 13).

Ever walk into a bank and see the suits running around stressed out, phones ringing, shouting across desks? Of course not. You could take your yoga mat into any bank and meditate in the middle of the lobby with a hot matcha tea. It's peaceful. It's calm. It's quiet. That silence is sound banking strategies at work.

Bankers don't need to fret. They use math and make passive income every minute.

This is why you don't see TV shows where the ensemble cast works at a bank. How boring would that be? Viewers want drama and stress. They want lawyers, cops, advertising executives, and the occasional medieval beheading before winter arrives.

You want boring when it comes to your money. Boring slides into the background and cranks away, like it should. Boring just doesn't have to be measly. Boring can be extremely profitable. And that just sounds more exciting than a beheading.

I want you to make a lot of monthly, passive income. I can only give you the fishing rod and show you how to cast it. Approaching the pond is up to you. Just don't get a bigger fishing boat because of it. That's what the majority does, and It defeats the purpose.

If you want to have wealth, don't flaunt it. And please don't buy the Lambo.

It's just business. Run it like one.

Run it like a bank if you want to *Make Bank.*

2

How To Become A Loan Shark

"Success is going from failure to failure
with no loss of enthusiasm."

- (attributed to) Winston Churchill

My own analogy as a way to think about money is influenced by too many business books to count. I service it, and regularly share it with others.

Here it is: Every dollar bill I have is a hired employee at my company. I picture the paper dollar with a little cartoon face, feet, hands, etc. Maybe it's holding a shovel or pick axe.

In this analogy I'm the animated factory honcho with a cigar looking over a huge Amazon-like warehouse of millions of workers. I run a tight ship, just like Jeff Bezos.

When I see one of my employees working successfully, I reward them. When I see one sitting idle or goofing around, I transfer them.

Apparently I'm not a bad boss because I don't fire them as often (or as loudly) as Donald Trump seems to. Rather, I willingly find a different department in my imaginary empire that might suit their skills better.

$1,000 sitting in an account realizing no gains is a set of 1,000 couch potatoes staring at the break room TV. They are not profitable for my factory. They are lethargic procrastinators taking up space and enjoying the complimentary snacks a tad too much. So I need to help them wipe the ketchup off their faces and fulfill their purpose of improving the taste of french fries. Oh yeah, my factory makes french fries. I figure, in good times or bad, who doesn't like a good fry? Economic immunity.

Everyone can feel passionate and energized when their skills are properly utilized. They feel appreciated. So, as the leader, I take responsibility when I ignore and don't nurture their potential.

Similarly, if I have $5,000 in a stock that is earning over 10% a year in dividends, I have adept employees. These 5,000 workers have found their calling - for that I reward them with tenure. Or I offer to promote them upstairs to a position with vertical potential (more than 10%), and of course a nice view of the bustling city.

When I consider buying something, I ask myself, "Is this thing that I'm about to buy worth pink-slipping 900 employees over?" Those 900 employees who can produce around the clock will be gone if I buy this shiny beach cruiser for $900. Do I really need it? My old one just needs a $50 tune-up. I'd rather furlough 50 employees than 900. Besides, the beach will weather that new shine in a couple weeks.

When you have money anywhere that isn't earning, it's burning. That money is a crew of employees you need to review. How have they benefited you? How can they make you more money? Today, I have clients who text me, "Where should I put my employees?" I chuckle that the metaphor has aged well.

There was a period when I produced a TV series in Burbank for Showtime called *Family Business*. At one point, the show was so dialed in, and limited to the talent's spotty schedule, that there wasn't much to do on days we weren't shooting. And I'm not one to sit with frivolous videos of cats riding the Roomba on YouTube, at least not after the 29th refresh of diminishing returns.

Having formally studied business, I was confident and conservative with my investments. I was doing fine on paper. But the stock market was up and down. I didn't receive steady income in the short-term with any regularity unless I was fortunate enough to produce a movie or TV show, flip a house, or hustle a side-hobby.

Real estate, as much as I love it, can be a lot of physical work if you don't leverage properly. I sweated many waking hours knocking down walls, learning to tile, and engaging in a scavenger hunt through hardware aisles weekend nights.

I caught the real estate up-cycles at the right time, flipping my first four houses. But those payouts were spread out years apart. The financial strategy was about appreciation. And I appreciated that. But it was stressful, arduous, and temporary. I knew it could end at any time.

It's no secret that people in Hollywood generally make very good fees. But it's also no secret that it's feast or famine. You can only eat what you hunt.

A hiatus can be long in Hollywood, with sporadic work contingent on competition and talent. If you're in the entertainment industry without other avenues for income, you're held hostage to gatekeepers and whims of that market.

I suspect this is no different than other industries.

So in between those vacuum-riding cat videos, I wanted a money stream that generated income, not just long-term wealth.

Craigslist's no-nonsense website was (and still is) valuable. I saw so much opportunity in this no-frills digital bulletin board. I posted an ad in the Financial Services section writing that I was making loans.

"Need Money? Contact me."

I know you're already shaking your head. I deserve that.

My first deal was with a guy who needed $1,000 for just one week. I charged 10%. So one week later he would return $1,100. Not a huge profit, but a colossal return. That 10% in one week is equivalent to 520% a year!

This was part of my strategy: optics.

Carl Richards, who spent more than 40,000 hours as a financial advisor at

Merrill Lynch and Wells Fargo said, "People who understand interest, earn it. People who don't, pay it."

If I'd said, "Okay, here's your $1,000 loan, and I'm charging you a 520% annual percentage rate (APR)," I'd never close the deal. But saying, "Hey, that will just be a hundred bucks," seemed reasonable.

The week went by, then two, then three. Suddenly 520% didn't matter. I was happy to take 0%. I just wanted my employees to return to the factory. Field trip over.

"I am not so much concerned with the return ON capital
as I am with the return OF capital."

Will Rogers

An important part of investing is simply not losing in the first place. Many investors would be so much better off if they did everything possible to not lose money. But we get greedy. We conflate action with results. And we lose to stupidity or impatience. That was me.

Warren Buffett is famous for his two rules:

1. Never lose money.

2. Never forget rule #1.

I have forgotten rule #2 on numerous occasions.

I unfortunately learned about the small claims process, filing a lawsuit, and serving a defendant. It was disheartening to spend additional money chasing my money. I feared I might be pouring good money after bad.

About 3 months later, I received an email from the borrower, yelling at me (it contained exclamation marks). He wrote that I didn't have to send the sheriffs to his parents' house at 4 am, wake everyone in a panic, and embarrass him.

I authorized the Santa Monica courthouse to have local sheriffs serve him the lawsuit after he ghosted me. When or how they do it is out of my hands.

Nevertheless, the message was loud and clear (the cops were *my* exclamation points). His parents paid me back $1,000 principal, plus $100 interest, plus a $300 late penalty, plus court costs (about $225).

Success!

But many of the stories don't end this way, as I would soon find out.

There was the single-mom who needed a breast reduction. She borrowed $5,000 for the surgery that would save her back. I guess her exotic dancing was weighing her down.

There was the student who needed $2,000 to complete his last semester of community college. I recall he was studying finance, come to think of it.

There was the guy with the "extremely valuable" antique camera collection who needed $4,000. Apparently, it was so valuable that I didn't need to verify his claim. He insisted I trust him. I did.

I met the borrowers at my local UPS office to get loan documents notarized. I copied their driver's licenses, and often required pre-filled out and signed checks endorsed to me for the loan's future payments. And I even took photos of them holding the contract and their IDs. Not bad precautions for someone about to lose all their money.

I was a bad judge of character in this world of loan-sharking, often swayed by a person's necessity rather than ability to pay me back. Some borrowers, regardless what they legally agree to, or what collateral they put up, are going to scam you anyway. I must have had a target on my ad.

The reason borrowers need funds is probably the least important thing. Yet, to this day, that's mostly all I remember: the story why they needed the funds. That overshadowed their credibility.

Needless to say - I'll say it because I can now finally laugh about it - all these borrowers fled the state, had fake I.D.s, or put up collateral worth less than they claimed (much less in the case of the antique cameras. Apparently "broken" doesn't equate to "antique").

Years later I would go on to produce 83 episodes of a TV show, *Auction Hunters*, where I learned just how critical expert verification and authentication are.

As you can imagine, this brought out the most shady characters I've ever dealt with. And I've dealt with personalities between Sunset and Mulholland. This was worse, more stressful, and lacked a gorgeous dusk view over an infinity pool.

When I add up the small wins from decent people who truly were who they said they were, I barely made a profit. Most borrowers needed roughly $300 and returned $350 just two weeks later. I had maybe four dozen of those. Not much money to write home about, but still, that's 1,733% APR.

Thankfully, those extreme usury rates wiped out the losses. But they also wiped out my time. And you unfortunately can't get a refund for wasted time.

I operated like an inefficient/ineffective bank, offering loans at high enough rates to cover the losses. But the math wasn't sustainable.

The police officers and law clerks at the courthouse were starting to recognize me. I would leave the edit room in Burbank to appear before a judge on the Westside to plead my case. No defendant ever showed up. I won by default every time.

Even the judge was starting to smirk when he'd see me walk into the courthouse. He probably knew what I was up to. Or maybe needed a loan himself.

Of course, winning a case is one thing. Collecting is another. And that's when I put my baseball bat and Tony Soprano tank top back in the drawer.

It was time to pull out the banker's suit. Cue heroic score.

3

Profit From Peer Pressure

"Debt is one person's liability, but another person's asset."

Paul Krugman

I spoke with an attorney about my lending activity to see if he could recommend a better way to protect myself while providing personal loans.

The first thing he pointed out was I was charging usury rates, which is completely illegal. Oops. In California, the maximum one is allowed to charge anyone is 10% per year. My 1,733% per year came in above that. Slightly.

If the borrowers had known to argue my egregious and illegal rates in court (had they appeared), they could have negated the loan by *charging me* with usury. Ignorance spared me.

Banks, credit card companies, and payday loan services that litter dilapidated strip malls can skirt these restrictions. They have the proper commercial and financial licenses that allow them to avoid usury ceilings. This is why you see credit card rates of 29.99% (30% is outrageous, but 29.99% is acceptable) and same-day pay services at 450%.

The attorney pointed out a loop-hole, wherein a real estate *broker* could lend to someone and charge any rate they want if the borrower's real estate is used as collateral.

Earlier, I had seen the value of obtaining a broker's license to build a side business writing mortgages for colleagues in the film and TV business. Since most of Hollywood is composed of freelancers and craftsmen, they aren't considered employees. They don't have regular income documented by W2s. Without consistent 3rd-party payroll, banks get confused over how someone could afford to buy a home (bankers are the opposite of Hollywood producers on the creative scale). I noticed this missing piece since I was in this same self-employed boat.

For my lending side-hustle this meant I could now lend to borrowers who already owned a home and charge north of the 10% ceiling. I could additionally put a lien on their house to secure my loan. No more worthless camera bodies collecting dust in my garage.

I wrote this narrative into a NatGeo pilot I produced, *Million Dollar Gamble*, about a collector who buys a van-full of antique cameras only to find out they're worthless. Apparently the pilot was worthless, too.

But after pursuing two deals, this proved to be too time consuming. Plus, borrowers who owned homes weren't willing to put their house on the line for a mere $5,000 bucks. They wanted loans of $100,000. That I couldn't do.

So that was the end of Craigslist banking for me. It was an experience and lesson that fortunately left me with a few cringeworthy tales to tell over a drink. Or at least include in a book.

I was back to saving conservatively, dollar-cost-averaging into safe mutual funds via my retirement account at Vanguard.

I focused on developing my movies, dipping my toe into TV, my mortgage hustle, and rehabbing homes.

But then 2005 rolled around. It was as if that year saw exactly what I was trying to do and said, "Oh, you poor bastard. I can help you." I was able to finally take my first baby steps into the *real* lending world, just like a bank.

If you're already familiar with peer-to-peer (P2P), feel free to play your get-out-of-this-chapter card and progress to the next one, chapter 4. There's a reason this is the shortest chapter in the book.

Or, stay for the ride. There are some financial nuggets and context that will come into play later.

P2P lending sites are the gateway drug of choice for the banking journey. I have since ventured much deeper (you will too) and identified more appealing and rewarding situations.

But this is the starting point if you are new to the world of lending. The critical criteria is similar and necessary for the other more advanced ones. Because in the end, all lending ultimately uses similar analytics.

Prosper and LendingClub, the U.S.'s first two available peer-to-peer lending websites, are robust, user-friendly, and anyone can become an instant banker with as little as $25 in cash. The path to becoming a banking baron is short and straight here.

These P2P sites alone won't make you rich. Let me make that clear. But they will extricate you from the inexplicable low rates a retail bank pays you. So as the first location to begin building your waterfall of cash, start with P2P to collect the necessary tools.

"How many millionaires do you know who have become wealthy by investing in savings accounts? I rest my case."

- Robert G. Allen

P2P gives consistently decent interest rates without lifting a finger. Actually, you do have to lift a finger to click a button. And then maybe the other fingers to type in the loan amount. But it doesn't require much more than that.

In 2008, when the financial crisis hit, the perfect storm catapulted P2P into the mainstream. Banks were required to have larger reserves and more strict lending standards. And, due to the crisis, there was a huge demand for loans. But banks were imploding, consolidating, and merging. Chances are you now bank at a place you didn't originally sign up at.

On the other end of the banking spectrum sat shady payday loan centers offering horrifically high rates. People didn't have a lot of choices. Which is the lesser evil?

When borrowers need to consolidate their credit cards, increase their cash flow, reduce their car loans, student loans, or even medical bills, where do they go outside of a bank or sketchy fast-cash business? Well, for over a decade, they've had numerous choices. That's where you as the banker comes in.

Both P2P sites are endorsed by many financial professionals and institutions. In fact a lot of institutional retirement and pension funds flow into these platforms. Their vetting process is so conservative and consistent that municipalities and Wall Street trust the numbers.

Here's how it works: Individuals or small business borrowers looking for any type of loan from as little as $500 - or up to $40,000 - can apply. The platforms approve/disapprove in a matter of days, not weeks. After the obligatory details (credit, background, employment, debt, etc.), they grade the loans and post them online for any investor to take all or fractions of the loan, sharing proportionately in the loan's proceeds or defaults.

Someone graded "A" may have really good credit and need a small loan compared to their income. Their borrowing rate (or your lending rate) may be as low as 5.5%. Other borrowers might have terrible credit but be able to prove their worth in other ways such as business cash flow. They might receive a "D" grade and pay as much as 13%.

Now take those two loans and add them to hundreds more. That's the kind of volume you can access and diversify into. Rather than risk $5,000 on the guy with the fake I.D. whom I spent 6 days emailing back and forth on Craigslist, I could now spread that over 200 different loans at $25, with varied risk levels and interest rates.

It sounds like a lot of work. But it's only work if you want the work out of curiosity. I was curious for the first 6 months, so I examined the loans carefully, reading every detail on the borrowers.

Today, I automate everything (as do most lenders) with bots that comb the deals and invest when my curated criteria is met. At this point, I have no idea until I check my statements once a year how many loans I've committed to or how much money I'm making. It smoothly runs in the background, the way a banker likes it.

As time goes on, and hundreds or thousands of these loans pay off, your cash account is replenished with your principal and interest. You can keep rolling over the proceeds into new loans, or transfer back to your linked checking account.

There will be defaults. There will be late payments. These platforms have that covered, too. They have a suite of collection agencies and a system to contact and work with the borrower before eventually writing them off, if need be (which you in turn get to write off).

The high volume and diversification achieved with artificial intelligence essentially guarantees you won't lose your principal. I've never heard of anyone who is diversified across numerous baskets of loans lose the amount of their investment. The whole point here is to spread that risk across numerous loans rather than have one $25,000 loan that defaults. At $25 minimums, if that's the most you put into any one loan, you would have 1,000 loans instead of one.

For instance, as of today, I've funded and had my principal returned on 25,242 loans on Prosper, and 12,309 loans on Lending Club. The sheer number is startling. But by rolling over closing loans into new ones, it doesn't take long to reach a high volume.

Many loans pay off early, sometimes within a month, and that capital is loaded into the next loan. So just one $25 investment that pays off every 3 months would be equivalent to 8 loans over a 2-year period if that was reinvested. Over 15 years this rolling snowball grows bigger and bigger.

Of those 37,551 loans, I've had 4,214 loans default, go into bankruptcy, or the borrower dies. So, a fairly high default rate of 11%.

There are various strategies on how to approach bad loans. I veer toward the conservative side. I join loans mostly with Grades A, B, and C, and shorter terms of three years or less. The maximum loan term is five years, but most are two years or less.

Others bankroll risky and speculative loans like Grade D or HR (High Risk). Those pay more - in the 12+ percentage range. These borrowers might have low credit scores, high debt, or other blemishes making them sub-prime. Yet, for lenders of these loans, the high interest rates outweigh the higher defaults.

Some of these lenders document their portfolios and strategies online and are doubling what I am earning, even with over 20% defaults. Take this approach with caution as I don't have personal experience with it.

Someone I know invested more aggressively and did not do so well; the loans turned out to be risky, and his yields were actually negative in the short term (they have since averaged above 4%).

The painless, straightforward solution may just be to employ a recommended portfolio allocation. These sites will flowchart you through your risk temperament and help you allocate your funds across a weighted basket of loans. They'll even forecast what kind of returns you can expect based on the weightings. It's akin to making your own mutual fund of loans.

Prosper and Lending Club will declare investors are averaging 5-9% on their loans (varies with the economy and fed rates). I used to get much higher rates, when I first started out. But after accounting for defaults and a declining economy, I'm currently averaging only 4.2% between the two sites.

Again, though, I take a conservative approach, perhaps too much so, missing out on the higher risk ones that might have better returns. But for someone just starting out who has money in a retail bank at .01%, this is 420x higher.

And that's how I mainly view this P2P space: as the 1st floor entrance to the bank lobby. This is where my first-day employees land to fill out paperwork with their freshly ironed suits before I figure out where to place them. In the meantime, I want them to make me at least *a little* something. P2P, for me, is that: a little something.

Want only one of these sites to start out? I'd pick LendingClub. They have a great ethos, education on finance, and customer support is superb, should you ever need it (you likely won't).

Here's a referral link that will help us both out: http://terencemichael.com/lendingclub.html

Now, it's time to don your black trench coat and leap from P2P into the Matrix, where you can earn *over double* what you can here.

4

Stabilize Income With A Coin

"Do not go where the path may lead,
go instead where there is no path and leave a trail."

- Ralph Waldo Emerson

What if I told you there was a simple and secure way to effortlessly earn at least 8.6% interest on your savings account? No minimums. No maximums. No hold periods. You can withdraw anytime.

That 8.6% is 860 times higher than what you're earning with the average retail savings account of .01% (Bank of America, Chase, and Wells Fargo are all paying .01% at time of publishing).

Put another eye-opening way: It will take over 2 years and 4 months to earn the same amount of interest you can in 1 day with this strategy I'm going to share.

Now sharing, because sharing is caring: http://terencemichael.com/blockfi.html

1. Sign up at BlockFi.

2. Buy USDC (United States Dollar Coin)

3. You're now earning 8.6%.

If you're happy with that and believe ignorance is bliss (I don't judge), then skip ahead two chapters to chapter 6. You're welcome. You just swallowed the Blue pill.

If you want to know more and potentially earn over double that 8.6%, take the Red pill and learn about the stable answer to our unstable banking system.

This newer world exists by lending "coins," that aren't actual coins, to people you don't know. They're liquid, secure, safe, and grow your funds passively.

They're called "stablecoins."

You've certainly heard of cryptocurrencies like Bitcoin, Ether, or Litecoin.

Bill Gates said, "Bitcoin is a technological tour de force." But Warren Buffett condemned it when he called it, "... rat poison squared." Either way, it's a financial inaccuracy to confuse stablecoins with Bitcoin. They do not share the same risk in any way, shape or form.

The same was also said about the internet when people thought it was nothing more than a dictionary or way to send letters to your college professor.

Nobel Prize-winning economist Paul Krugman said back in 1998, "It will become clear that the Internet's impact on the economy has been no greater than the fax machine's." Paul Krugman was wrong. And I strongly believe Warren Buffett will be proven wrong too.

Plus, we're talking about something very different.

Stablecoins live in the cryptocurrency universe on the Ethereum blockchain. You don't have to know what that means, other than that it exists on a massive, decentralized, digital ledger in a more efficient, alternate money system that is the fastest growing asset class in the last decade. This ledger and all of its recorded transactions are open-source and available for anyone in the world to verify and confirm.

These "coins" operate and function as a bridge to the traditional financial foundation. This is why they're deemed "stable." Unlike the extreme volatility of Bitcoin and Ether, stablecoins are a tokenized version of fiat (U.S. Dollar, euro, yen, or any country's issued currency).

If you just purchased $50 worth of a stablecoin such as USDC from BlockFi, you will always be able to turn around and sell that USDC stablecoin for exactly $50. Hold it for 10 minutes or 10 years, it will never go up or down compared to the currency it is tethered to. 1 USD = 1 USDC. And 1 USDC = 1 USD. Stable.

On the lower end of the interest scale (6-8.6% range), your only necessary action is to buy stablecoins with a trusted, centralized company that behaves as your custodian.

On the higher end of the interest scale (9-20% range), you deposit with specific, short-term hold periods, so it's slightly less liquid. And there's another wrinkle, but easy to iron out. More on this later.

In both cases, you collect interest. And in both cases you can make a lot of passive income, because there isn't anything more for you to do other than sit back with an umbrella to shield you from the money that will rain on you.

Let's back up a minute to further understand the crypto-verse. Because if you haven't joined Neo and Morpheus yet, this sounds too crazy good to be true.

How can a parallel financial world exist right under us that is blowing the doors off our known, traditional banking system in terms of interest rates? Wouldn't everyone be flocking to this? Especially with doors missing?

Cash is dirty, slow, and awkward. If you're standing next to your best friend and need to pay them 50 bucks and happen to have 50 bucks on you, you can hand it to them right there. Now you no longer owe them from last Thursday night's poker game. Transaction complete.

But what if you don't have 50 bucks in your pocket at the time you suddenly bump into your friend in the frozen aisle at Trader Joe's? What if you just purchased 50 dollars worth of gas station scratch-offs as a poor plan for "winning back" your poker losses? Unless that's the last 50 dollars to your name, you still *have* 50 dollars, somewhere. But you can't transfer it to your friend because you don't have a horizontal green piece of paper representing that 50 bucks.

But you are you. And your friend is your friend. And you are both standing there. Why can't you transfer 50 dollars worth of value from your ownership to theirs, especially if you both agree to it?

What if, six days later, you finally give your now ex-friend 50 dollars, but they later say you never did? Did you bump your head? Do you need an MRI? Where's the proof?

What if you really do have amnesia and turns out you actually owe $5,000, not $50, from the worst bluff of poker you've ever performed in Texas hold 'Em? Now you're relegated to wiring the money. That takes an appointment with a banker, paperwork, thumbprints, fees, and usually days (if not an entire week) to transfer. In the meantime, your ex-friend is parked outside your house with some of his larger friends. Looks like they came from batting practice.

What if you want to convert the only $5,000 to your name into euros or any other country's denomination because you realize you better get out of town until this blows over? Or what if you need to borrow $5,000 from someone else to make this go away, but they want to collect interest from you?

The answers to all of these questions is time, money, and an intermediary. Not to mention finding new friends.

You're familiar with Facebook's Libra, so you already know one popular stablecoin. Facebook wants to have a borderless, instantaneous monetary system so that everyone who has a Facebook profile can transact with each other without dependence on third parties. What they've done for sharing photos, stories, and videos they are doing for cash transactions.

Of course, Facebook being Facebook, the government is skeptical and nervous of such a ubiquitous monopoly from someone who started out wanting to compare college girls to barnyard animals. This is why they are also scared of (but taking baby steps into) digital money. They're concerned about becoming obsolete.

Any type of alternate money system dilutes the government's control. They want full authority to adjust the money supply, value or devalue the dollar, and manipulate the economy (for good or bad). This grants them the keys to the world's money dashboard. They just don't always drive sober.

Many people believe this is overreaching. They want jurisdiction over their own hard-earned money. They want to make their own choices. They want to know that if $3 buys a carton of eggs today, it won't be $5 tomorrow due to devaluation. They also want to be in the driver's seat, and put the drunk government in the back to dry out.

The purchasing power of $1 in 1913 has now diminished to less than 8 cents today. And it got much worse with the largest quantitative easing and stimulus packages the world had ever seen after COVID-19. This is why you can't store your money in a safe or a bank. It evaporates over time.

You would've been better off in 1935 buying as many Monopoly board games as you could for $2 apiece rather than putting that same amount of money in the bank. Each 1935 Monopoly game's play money is today worth over $50 to collectors. But $2 in the bank in 1935 is today less than 20 cents.

When you go to the arcade and buy tokens to play games, you are engaging in a small form of pseudo stablecoin. You know how much the games cost, so you know what the tokens are worth. You can off-ramp from the arcade and on-ramp into the real world with your money.

Ditto for a Las Vegas casino. You can exchange back and forth into and out of their branded chips all you want (perhaps the safest bet in Vegas). You are confident in the value as long as you trust the casino.

This is called tokenization. It's really an archaic term brought into the virtual future to digitize money. Because, again, cash is impractical for most transactions in the world. Therefore if a company issuing those tokens can be trusted and remains stable in value, you have a stablecoin.

The risk is that someone steals your tokens. The video arcade isn't FDIC insured. The casino isn't FDIC insured. You have to be careful where you set your casino chips when ordering a single-malt scotch, neat. And there's risk the video arcade will go out of business due to insufficient retro Donkey Kong consoles (who didn't see that coming?).

If you're stuck with those tokens or casino chips, who else will take them? Will other casinos accept the defunct casino's chips? Will a competing arcade honor the other arcade's tokens?

Were Facebook to announce they would no longer honor the Libra coin, there would be a mass riot. But the risk is highly unlikely due to the network effect, utility value, and global adoption. It's no different than paper money. Physical dollar bills only have value because we say they have value, and everyone accepts this story. It's a cooperative narrative we all subscribe to.

You and your friends are already shuffling 1s and 0s back and forth to reimburse each other with Venmo, PayPal, CashApp, or the bank's Zelle system. You're not really using physical cash. You're merely using digital versions.

But PayPal doesn't issue PayPal Dollars. Venmo doesn't issue Venmo coins. What would you do with those? Unless hundreds and thousands of merchants agreed to accept Venmo coins, there's no point in saving Venmo coins. There's also no conversion with these companies. You can't Venmo to PayPal, or CashApp to Zelle. They don't play in the same sandbox.

As efficient as current payment apps have become, they still charge fees and have delays. When you go to take ownership of actual physical cash, it's not fast or free. Yet it's your money.

Payment apps are also bordered by politics and geography. You can't effortlessly send money to relatives in another country. You can only sign up with these apps if you have a bank account. And many people still pay exorbitant fees to send via antiquated merchants like Western Union or MoneyGram.

Most of the world's population is unfortunately unbanked. They are disadvantaged from starting their own businesses, receiving money and loans, and enjoying leverage of the worldwide economy. There's no liquidity or arbitrage for them. They should be able to access micro loans, grants, and sell goods and services without a barter system trading woolly mammoth meat for cave art.

With stablecoins, and with crypto in general, it takes nano-seconds and goes straight from sender to receiver - no middlemen, unless you want such. Superior features include ease of use, interface, security. All you need is access to the Internet, available in any Internet cafe in any 3rd world country.

It's no surprise that those apps above now incorporate crypto into their payment systems. The Square app, PayPal, and Venmo all offer their users onramps to Bitcoin. Change is definitely coming.

Imagine how efficient buying a home will soon be. It won't have to take 30 days and mountains of paperwork. Ditto for tracking business inventory, authenticating products, tracing vaccines, issuing intellectual property, etc.

Want to use a musician's song in your little youtube video but you don't have the rights? What if you could pay 7.5 cents, which goes straight to the artist?

What if you don't want to subscribe to *The Wall Street Journal* or *The New York Times*, but you'd happily pay 3 cents to read one article? What about just one Hulu or one HBO episode for 72 cents? And 12 cents for a repeat viewing?

How do you know the yellowtail sushi that just arrived at your restaurant is less than 18 hours old from catch to plate? How do you know that's a real Gucci? Or real Air Jordans? Or a genuine Rolex? Tokenization solves this.

Crypto, coins, and tokens basically change the paradigm of time and money. For example, if someone performs a job and they're salaried $2,000 a week, why do they have to wait until the end of the week to get *their* $2,000? It's already legally theirs, incrementally, as they work, at $400 a day, or $50 an hour, or 83 cents a minute, or 1.38 cents a second.

We're so accustomed to this pay delay that no one questions it. This lag time is no different than waiting for a bank wire to process. Someone else is earning interest off your money. But tokenization will soon change this. At any moment in time you'll be able to access an app and see your salary meter accumulating. You can then press a button with a debit account attached to your phone and buy whatever you need, when you need to.

This is one of the main reasons Satoshi Nakamoto wrote the seminal white paper and birthed Bitcoin back in October of 2009 amidst the financial crisis. He (or "they"; no one but Satoshi knows for sure) envisioned a future that didn't depend on these integrated institutions, like the government and banks. Thus the birth of Bitcoin, which birthed cryptocurrencies, which birthed a massive demand for stablecoins.

Whereas the P2P space (from the last chapter) is transacting about $85 billion in annual volume after being around for 15 years, stablecoins are already doing over $10 billion at less than 2 years old.

There are 9 major, global stablecoins, most of which are widely accepted on all crypto exchanges throughout the world, 24/7, and with complete price parity to fiat - USDC, GUSD, SAI, DAI, BUSD, HUSD, Pax USD, USDT, and TUSD. Again, all 1 to 1.

You don't have to remember all those. I focus solely on USDC and GUSD.

USDC (United States Dollar Coin) was created by Coinbase and Circle. These two behemoth crypto companies effectively formed a massive crypto bank that creates and issues these coins. You can then buy them almost anywhere, like Coinbase, BlockFi, or dozens of other exchanges. They also happen to have some of the best interest rates due to their ubiquity.

For every USDC that is created when you purchase one, 1 U.S. dollar is deposited into their bank (a consortium called CENTRE) that is assigned to your stablecoin. This is how they guarantee, without fractional banking, that when you have 1 USDC there will always be 1 actual physical U.S. dollar for you to exchange.

They're not creating these coins out of thin air, like the government does with their federal printing machine.

My second favorite stablecoin is GUSD (Gemini United States Dollar). It's much smaller in market cap than USDC, but has similar safety, security, and protocols behind it.

Gemini is a FinTech (Financial Technology) exchange created by Cameron and Tyler Winklevoss. The Winklevii, as they are plurally known, are twin Geminis, ex-Olympian rowers, and you might recall them as the original pioneers of Facebook as played by Armie Hammer, twice, in the Oscar-nominated movie, *The Social Network*.

Gemini has become the market leader for custodial services in crypto, including stablecoins. In fact, their exchange is the technical custodian for all BlockFi's stablecoins. So even though I own both USDC and GUSD on the platform BlockFi, all is safely secured by Gemini's cold storage (offline, away from hackers).

The Winklevii come from traditional, East Coast Wall Street finance. They're raised and steeped in old school, conservative financial models. They formed their exchange in hopes of being the main gateway for analog bankers to finally get into Bitcoin. They're paving that path quickly and may soon launch the first official U.S. Bitcoin ETF. My money is on them.

If you're up for a fantastic read, check out Ben Mezrich's book, *Bitcoin Billionaires*. It's the true-life 2nd act followup to the 1st act they had with Facebook. It picks up where *The Social Network* ended when the Winklevii received their $65M 2008 settlement from Mark Zuckerberg due to their original HarvardConnect idea. Zuckerberg turned it into The Facebook, and eventually just Facebook.

With a tiny fraction of that settlement the Winklevii purchased Bitcoin that is worth over $2 billion today (they own 210,000 Bitcoins), making them the first Bitcoin billionaires.

I suspect Tyler and Cameron will have the last laugh in the history books. Do you think it's any surprise Zuckerberg has now created a stablecoin named Libra *after* the Winklevii already created one first called Gemini? Give that some thought. I would join in and create Scorpio, but I didn't attend Harvard.

The easiest way to buy GUSD is to simply convert some of the USDC you purchased on BlockFi to GUSD. You can convert these two into the other 1 to 1 all day long at zero cost. Why? My brain tells me it's generally good to diversify. But really, both of these are with quality teams and strict compliance. So it probably doesn't matter.

You could also buy GUSD at its main home, Gemini. Here's a link: http://terencemichael.com/gemini.html. You can also buy and exchange the main cryptocurrencies like Bitcoin, Ether, and Litecoin. But as far as stablecoins go, you can eliminate a step by simply purchasing GUSD at BlockFi where the interest rates are high. BlockFi will store them at Gemini in the background without your having to have a Gemini account.

If you're content with owning stablecoins and collecting interest, you've succeeded with this chapter. But if you want to know more, if you're curious how this all works and why it is the fastest growing sector in finance, venture further in the next chapter where we go one level deeper into this lucrative framework.

5

Give Leverage To Speculators

"There's a big industry around Bitcoin.
It is volatile, but people make money off volatility."

- Richard Branson

Because the crypto industry is still so young, there isn't enough volume to stabilize the wild fluctuations in the markets. Bitcoin's price can go up or down over 100% in a year (sometimes as much as 30% intraday).

It won't always be this way. But today it is. Today it's a roller coaster on steroids. And that's why you, the "banker," get to benefit from these wild gyrations.

As more financial startups, pension and retirement funds, foundations, family offices, hedge funds, and endowments enter the space, this volatility will shrink. More on-ramps are surfacing. Institutions like Fidelity, Goldman Sachs, and JP Morgan are offering exposure via funds and pseudo-ETFs. Soon crypto will become as ubiquitous as gold, which is why it's often referred to as "digital gold."

Fidelity Investments reported that over a third of institutional investors in the U.S. and Europe have slowly and quietly been stacking Bitcoin and Ether. They've been quietly buying digital assets at an increasing rate every year over the past four years. Due to crypto's stigma (similar to the internet's early days), very few traditional investment firms are publicly announcing their exposure to it.

For now, however, the problem is that gyrations and volatility are sometimes off the charts. When I started contemplating this book, Bitcoin was at $6,800 after taking a slow dive over two years to $4,000. I first started buying in late 2017 at $11,700, and watched it climb to almost $20,000. As of publishing, Bitcoin is now half that at $10,000. I'm sure by the time you read this, it won't be close to that. Again, too crazy and volatile to track your daily spending. Who would feel safe using it as a store of value with such gyrations?

This is why the space has attracted so many professional speculators. When you find securities and assets that move quickly in any direction, there is money to be made on spreads and arbitrage.

Traders - both personal and institutional - who time the market can't just let their crypto sit on exchanges in a crypto's denomination. Unlike the stock market, there's no break. The crypto world knows no holidays, doesn't differentiate weekends from weekdays, and doesn't care what time it is or which country you are from.

You can go to bed with one valuation and wake up with a completely different one. As bad as this is for the individual speculator, financial institutions who are trading billions of dollars worth of Bitcoin can't afford to let it sit idle. They immediately move it off the Bitcoin freeway into a safe, stable parking garage where no one can crash into it (and it isn't burning fuel).

This freeway is a 24/7 global infrastructure that everyone and every country is trafficking all at once. We've never had that before in a trading world of securities or property. Anyone with an Internet connection anywhere in the world can drive onto one of now hundreds of exchanges around the world and transact.

Most of these exchanges, especially foreign ones, only trade in cryptocurrencies. Therefore the only form of "cash" they have is stablecoins. If you want to buy Bitcoin, Ether, Litecoin, ChainLink or VeChain on exchanges outside of the U.S., you have to first send a stablecoin from your stablecoin wallet that you purchased on a platform like Coinbase or BlockFi into your stablecoin wallet on the foreign exchange of your choosing. Then you can buy whatever cryptocurrency you want with that stablecoin. These become a form of world-wide currency reinforcing their use-case.

Another utility of stablecoins, and the one that most impacts you as a lender, is a practical way for speculators to borrow money.

If a trader had been buying Bitcoin during the dips and has a low dollar-cost-average, they may not want to sell. Selling would trigger a capital gains tax. It would also disrupt their long-term intention of benefiting from the future growth of Bitcoin.

Selling also becomes expensive for a trader if they just want to take the *value* of their gains for outside opportunities. They may see profitable plays in real estate, stocks, or artwork. They have the value in Bitcoin to get into those vehicles, but they don't want to sell for the above reasons.

Rather, using the Bitcoin they own as collateral, they can borrow against it. This provides them with the liquidity they need elsewhere without unplugging from Bitcoin.

For example, let's say Rachel owns 5 Bitcoins. Let's say the current price is $10,000 per coin, for easy math. But she doesn't want to sell for several reasons. She thinks Bitcoin will quadruple within the next two years (I agree with Rachel), so she wants to hang onto her basis, since she purchased it at $3,700 a coin in January of 2019, back when I recommended people look into it on my podcast. If she sells, she incurs massive taxes and gives up future opportunities.

But that's not the only reason. Rachel also has a wedding coming up. She needs some cash for expenses, as well as cash for a down payment on an income property she wants to buy after having read chapter 8 of this book. Furthermore, she is so bullish on Bitcoin, she seeks leverage to buy even more.

By transferring her 5 Bitcoins to an asset-backed lending site like BlockFi, she instantly has collateral to borrow stablecoins against her 5 Bitcoins, currently valued at $50,000. And those stablecoins she borrows have price parity with her fiat, 1 to 1. Ultimately, it's cash she seeks.

Unlike P2P sites in chapter 3, there's no credit check. It's simple and instantaneous for her because she has the universally accepted collateral in crypto: Bitcoin. BlockFi can immediately confirm her wallet address on the blockchain and thus its value.

Similar to paper money Bitcoin is Bitcoin. No one Bitcoin is more valuable than another Bitcoin (for the most part. I could get very nerdy here with tainted addresses, but I can't find my extra thick glasses).

Like a pawn shop of sorts, BlockFi takes possession of Rachel's 5 Bitcoins. She still gains the benefit (or loss) of that Bitcoin as the value goes up or down within her secure wallet. But now only BlockFi holds the keys to that wallet. Only BlockFi can unlock it while it's hanging on the wall in their pawn shop.

BlockFi tells Rachel what amount she can borrow based on the LTV (Loan-To-Value) of her collateral. If the requirement is a 40% LTV (typical in this space), then she can borrow up to $20,000 of her $50,000 worth of Bitcoin (40% of $50,000 = $20,000). If it's 50%, then $25,000, and so on. BlockFi adjusts these LTVs judiciously as they monitor the volatility of the markets.

So with her $25,000 in USDC stablecoin, she can disconnect from the Matrix $25,000 U.S. dollars. She can now pay for her southern chic wedding, put a down payment on an income property, and buy additional Bitcoin. Yet she hasn't sold any of her original 5 Bitcoins. Rachel is a happy camper, and she doesn't even like camping.

If the Bitcoin market declines, however, BlockFi will notify her to either add more to her Bitcoin collateral position or pay down the loan. Or they'll even sell off some of her Bitcoin if she's non-responsive because she's dancing at her wedding to Kool & The Gang and also failed to splurge for the wedding dress with velcro phone pocket that would have held her ringing phone.

In any case, the LTV stays in the acceptable and agreed-upon range. BlockFi protects itself (and thus you, provider of these stablecoins) with collateral substantially worth more than the value they are lending.

BlockFi charges the borrower somewhere around 15%. This may sound ridiculously high to you. But the borrower is happy to pay that rate because she's a sophisticated trader.

Rachel knows that it would cost her 30% in capital gains taxes if she sold her Bitcoin. She'd also lose her buy-and-hold strategy for long-term growth. And, of course, there goes her downtown, rooftop wedding with the multi-drone lighting ceremony.

And this is just Rachel. Where the majority of the volume comes from is Rachel's maid-of-honor, Cynthia. Cynthia is a seasoned, sophisticated trader. She works for a major financial institution like Genesis, Galaxy, or some other firm that starts with "G." These FinTech firms move and make millions of Gs within hours. They do this with arbitrage.

Since there are hundreds of crypto exchanges all over the world, the price of Bitcoin isn't the same on each exchange. The price on any one exchange can only reflect the agreed-upon settlement based on the volume of sellers and buyers at that point in time.

Take a quick look at CoinMarketCap (https://coinmarketcap.com/currencies/bitcoin/markets) and scan down the Price column, you'll see Bitcoin's price can be different from one exchange to another by as much 20%. This price differential makes people like Cynthia salivate, which is messing up her bridesmaid dress.

By buying Bitcoin on one exchange and simultaneously selling it on another exchange at the exact same point in time, she makes the difference within seconds. But the only way to ensure it's happening at the exact same point in time is by borrowing and shorting with options to protect herself.

When crypto moves so fast in either direction, timing is critical. It can also prove highly profitable.

If Bitcoin is trading for $10,100 on Exchange A, but for $11,000 on Exchange B, there's a potential for $900 profit. Cynthia could buy it from Exchange A, transfer it to Exchange B, sell it, and then transfer into a stablecoin for the profits and concurrently avoid the price fluctuations after her trade.

But because Bitcoin fluctuates so quickly, she is exposed to risk of losing the opportunity, or even losing money. What if Exchange B's price suddenly drops below the $10,100 she paid over on Exchange A? Now she's scrambling just to lose less.

This is why Cynthia needs to borrow so she can place short options on Exchange B to have a floor price she's guaranteed at buying Bitcoin, just in case. It's insurance.

I don't want to get too granular with futures, shorting, and prediction markets. But suffice it to say that similar to regular stock and commodity trading in traditional Wall Street markets, the same leverage tools are used by Cynthia and her institutional friends in crypto. And we're talking billions of dollars in transactions.

One of the largest digital investment firms is Grayscale (another "G"!). They have a Bitcoin Trust that can be traded with major brokerages like Fidelity. You can even own it in your IRA and avoid trading taxes all together.

During a 10-day period in May, 2020, Grayscale purchased $189M worth of Bitcoin for their investors. With that level of activity, Grayscale is using stablecoins and arbitrage when they buy. They are making sure they get Bitcoin as cheap as possible, to maximize profits for their clients.

If Rachel's wedding budget goes over, Cynthia has her covered due to arbitrage and stablecoin borrowing. She was a good choice for Rachel's maid-of-honor.

BlockFi isn't the only game in town for digital, asset-backed lending. Other favorites of mine are:

- Celsius
- Nexo
- Voyager
- Cyrpto.com
- Coinbase

These are all custodian platforms. They are centralized, like a bank, so they take on lending risk. You don't lend directly to the borrower. Instead, you lend to a platform, who in turn lends to the borrower. This is called CeFi, or Centralized Finance, as opposed to DeFi, Decentralized Finance.

DeFi is also a fast growing industry wherein you loan directly to a borrower without an intermediary. But for the *Make Bank* life, I feel the industry is too nascent at this stage for me to recommend. It's open source and public which makes it slightly more vulnerable to hackers and user error. It's the future. You'll start hearing about it more and more because there's a lot of money to be made. But for *Make Bank*, I'm sticking with CeFi.

BlockFi - Founder Zac Prince has been in the lending and funding sector most of his life so going digital into crypto lending and wealth management is a natural transition. He has a high level team of portfolio and finance managers from traditional space like American Express and Credit Suisse. They are also aligned with the largest U.S. leaders in crypto from Coinbase to Gemini.

They have raised over $100M from other lending companies like SoFi, so they tend to pay the highest interest rates right now. I personally allocate most of my stablecoin deposits here, both USDC and GUSD. BlockFi Link: http://terencemichael.com/blockfi.html

Nexo - My favorite non-U.S. asset-backed lender is Nexo. They have been lending online since before Bitcoin even existed. And they're the first in crypto lending. Based in Switzerland, they use different vernacular, like "topping up" rather than "depositing."

Unlike BlockFi, you can lend in over 45 different crypto coins. At publishing they are paying lenders 8% on stablecoins. You can find them at Nexo.io (not .com).

Voyager - This is 100% app based. They currently only pay 6% on a couple of stablecoins, but it's a full exchange in the palm of your hand. You can buy, sell, and store all kinds of other crypto coins just like you can with Nexo.

Based in NYC, Silicon Valley executives from E*Trade and Uber, etc. formed this company. So, like BlockFi, I feel a certain allegiance to an American company I can contact. Voyager Link: http://terencemichael.com/voyager.html

Coinbase - This is one of the most solid, seasoned, and by far largest U.S. based crypto companies there is. It's a behemoth in terms of backers, investors, notoriety, adoption, volume, etc. They have a fantastic interface, easy user experience, and responsive customer service.

Coinbase, however, pays a pittance of only 1.25% on stablecoins, which is nothing in the world of Neo. But if your journey into crypto continues beyond stablecoins, you will inevitably be dealing with them.

It's a place I initially buy most of my Bitcoin and USDC, but then transfer elsewhere to convert and boost my profits. Coinbase link: http://terencemichael.com/coinbase.html

These next two companies represent a growing trend for lenders to earn much more than BlockFi's 8.6%, Nexo's 8%, or Voyager's 6%. That's because they are trying to grow their own *native coins,* and are willing to pay for that privilege.

It would be like Chase Bank offering their regular savings rate at .01%, but then additionally offering a whopping 5% if you were willing to accept interest in the form of a Chase Bank Coin instead of dollars. And actually, that's similar to what J.P. Morgan is developing with their own JPM Coin. Other banks will soon follow.

Celsius - Celsius is an example of this native coin offering. If you are willing to stake your stablecoins and additionally receive interest in their own personal CEL token, you can boost your interest rates to 12%+. But beware because these native tokens are also traded on exchanges, so they aren't stable. They fluctuate in value, just like Bitcoin. This can be good or bad, depending on price movement.

You do, however, have the option to earn in regular stablecoins just like BlockFi, and earn 8.69%. Celsius is a global company with offices in NYC,

London, and Tel Aviv. They have over 100,000 retail and 260 institutional clients in over 150 countries. In just two years they've originated over $8.2 billion in digital loans. Celsius link: http://terencemichael.com/celsius.html

Crypto.com - This Hong Kong based company is probably the most generous with its interest rates, but potentially also the most confusing. Like Celsius and Voyager, it's only app based. But you can earn extremely high rates of over 18% if you are willing to earn it in their native MCO coin. But you also have to first buy and stake (hold) a certain level of MCO coin to gain these extraordinary rates.

All of these platforms either have (or will have) Visa or Mastercard debit cards so you can effectively spend any of your crypto, whether stablecoin or Bitcoin, on any purchase anywhere in the world. Their credit card instantly converts your crypto so the merchant doesn't even know you're paying with Bitcoin or GUSD.

I'm personally waiting for BlockFi and Nexo's debit cards to be issued. I will be using those.

Crypto.com does offer the best rewards (interest rates), but having to stake their native MCO coin is off-putting, since that itself could decrease in value.

These cards are the next phase of crypto adoption. Because with stablecoins paying huge interest and then having the access and ease of a debit card, the question becomes, why not move from the slow and expensive fiat world to the efficient and inexpensive crypto one?

In the crypto universe you can save, earn, and spend efficiently and effectively while your money is working for you until the very second you need to fire it with a debit card..

All these companies have transparent, third party auditing; insurance for their deposits and storage; financial licensing; and other regulatory oversight. Each company is different, but each has their own unique guarantees, storage, and protocols to ensure your money is safe.

There is risk, as with anything in life. I have to say that, even though I hate saying it. There is user-error. There is theft. There are hackers, just as there is with your regular bank. So follow best practices and standards. Protect your passwords. Use 2FA (2nd Factor Authentication - I like Google's Authenticator app). And you'll be fine.

You can absolutely hate Bitcoin. You can hate crypto. You don't have to buy into this whole Keanu-Reeves-leaning-backwards-in-slow-motion money system. I get it. No one wants back problems and years of physical therapy.

But don't hate stablecoins, unless you hate making automatic and passive income that is at least 860 times higher than your bank currently pays.

6

Let Wall Street Pay You

"Do you know the only thing that gives me pleasure?
It's to see my dividends coming in."

- John D. Rockefeller

It's easy to pick winning stocks during a bull market.

A drunk monkey can throw a dart at the list of S&P 500 companies and any one of those will climb in value. If not, it will ultimately be replaced on the index - one reason index funds are efficient. They let the market work for you.

This gives investors false confidence in how they pick stocks for investment. We think hearing Elon Musk introduce his new CyberTruck or a successful rocket launch is reason enough to buy Tesla or SpaceX. Or a leak of Apple's new iPhone becomes a beacon to buy Apple.

During economic expansion and a robust economy those stocks will generally rise. We witness this and confirm our bias for stock selection. But we confuse causation with correlation. And sometimes skill with luck.

Day traders want movement and volatility. They buy the rumor (long before you've heard it) and sell the news (often before you read it). They're in and out sometimes 3 times a day making money on tiny margins with their technical analysis and charting.

But, as wealth builders, we know the inherent risks and taxable events when trading short-term. Prudent strategy can become expensive or even detrimental in hindsight. We know holding long-term is solid advice. It's how we ultimately buy low and sell high (or buy high and sell higher). Time flattens out the myopic gyrations.

It's been said that the best time to sell a stock is never. We have enough historical data to see how the market has weathered the storms, crashes, catastrophes, depressions, and even pandemics. Over time, it's always gone up. Always.

That's sound advice for long-term, generational appreciation. Even day-traders won't argue that. They can't. It's a fact. They just want to make money in the interim.

However, for strategies like a bank, we want to separately collect regular payouts, not just price appreciation. We want *dividends.*

Dividends are the rent checks of Wall Street. Stocks go up or down, just like real estate goes up or down. But dividends from the right stocks never stop, just like rent from good tenants never stops.

Many investors don't pay attention to dividends. Think about the stocks you own, either individually or as part of a mutual fund - can you distinguish which ones pay dividends and which ones don't? Do you know how much your dividend stocks pay out as dividends?

We fixate on the price. It's a quick metric. It's splashed on TV 24/7. Our brains enjoy numbers. They're comforting. They immediately reduce confusion and reveal a story.

But when economic contraction and recession set in, suddenly it's not so straightforward to pick winners. Where did all of your friends go who were boasting about their stock-picking prowess at the K-Cup coffee maker? Maybe they didn't like where the story was going.

Investors panic sell at a loss or incur a large capital gains tax, and miss out on a company's turnaround. But what if they were still getting monthly or quarterly checks, no matter the stock price?

Companies that consistently pay dividends are the ones you want for passive, static income. You receive modest cash flow so you don't have to fret as much about appreciation in the short-term.

With dividend stocks, a company knows it's important to shareholders to receive quarterly checks in exchange for investing in them. This is a stockholder's reward. As a company's revenue comes in each quarter, they pay off their expenses, retain a certain amount of earnings, and then share the wealth with a percentage of dividends.

If I buy an income property and it generates $1,000 a month for me for the rest of my life, I don't care so much whether the value of it goes up or down because I'm never selling. Why would I sell an automatic money machine like this? As long as that $1,000 a month continues I'm happy. What makes me happier is if that $1,000 a month increases annually, forever.

Here are some random companies which consistently pay out increasing dividends every year. I'm not personally endorsing them (my attorney is no fun). These stocks will prove my point:

Mercury Insurance (ticker: MCY) has been increasing their dividends to shareholders for 34 years straight with a yield of 6.26%.

Walgreens (WBA) has been doing this for 44 years at 4.3%.

Coca Cola (KO) has been increasing its dividend payouts for the last 57 years, with a yield currently at 3.59%.

The dividend yield is the annual dividend amount divided by the stock price.

Yield = Dividend / Stock Price

Or, Dividend = Stock Price x Yield

If Exxon Mobil (XOM), which has been paying increasing dividends consistently for over 37 years, is paying a current 8.5% yield and the stock prices is $43; then the dividend per share is $3.65 (8.5% x $43).

How can the dividends go up that many years in a row and the dividend yield rate be so low? Coca Cola's dividend yield is only at 3.59%, yet goes up every single year. That's because it's the total *amount* of dividend you receive that is increasing, not the percentage rate.

The dividend yield rate could actually be going *down*, but your total dividends are still going up. That's a good sign because it means that the share price must also be going up.

If you buy 1,000 shares of Walgreens at $43.50 per share and are getting a 4.3% dividend yield, that's $1,870.50 in dividends. But let's say next year the dividend yield *rate* drops to 3.5%. If the price of Walgreens stock has climbed to $53.50, then that's $1,872.50 in dividends, $2.50 more than the last payout. Walgreens has increased your dividends, even though the yield has decreased.

Therefore, don't get stuck on the actual yield *rate* when looking at dividends. If the company is increasing its dividends every year, that's the critical factor: dividend amount, not yield rate.

There are dividend stocks paying over 20% dividends. Sounds enticing. But if their share price is falling, 20% may be irrelevant. 20% of zero is still zero.

Some companies are growth companies. It's possible one of your favorite stocks is taking all of its profits after expenses and calling them "retained earnings." They plow that money back into research, expansion, and new technology. These are amazing companies for buy and hold investors who don't need income, but rather appreciation. Huge gains can be made here.

If monthly income is the focus, however, you want *income* companies, not necessarily *growth* companies. These are businesses which make cash from re-buyables, necessities, and consumables - not stuff of the future.

Just look at the companies above.

Walgreens isn't sending us to the moon. It's providing household staples that we continually need to replenish, like toothpaste, coffee filters, and paper towels. They just want to continue providing value and convenience, like their competitor CVS (Consumer Value Store).

Ditto with Coca Cola and its line of beverages. Likewise with ExxonMobil. These are all consumable products and commodities that we buy over and over again.

SpaceX (not public) is a growth company. They are trying to send us to space. And Tesla is transporting us in expensive, driverless cars. Both of Elon Musk's companies need every penny for research and innovation. For that, I'll invest in the future and see where this goes. I know it's a gamble.

But for current income, I want dividend companies. I want AT&T, which has increased their dividends for 36 consecutive years and is currently paying a yield of 5.4%.

It's important to observe that dividends are discretionary. No company has to pay dividends. It's exclusively up to its board of directors. But the culture of a company becomes clear by looking at its historical record.

For some the decision to pay dividends is the cost of doing business and keeping loyal shareholders. For others paying dividends is a waste of cash, which should be pumped back into the company.

There are Qualified and Ordinary Dividends. You want the Qualified ones. For the most part, this just means: hang onto your stocks. Don't day-trade, don't jump in and out of them, or you'll be penalized with excessive taxes.

When you are trying to time the market or exactly when the company is issuing dividends, the IRS is going to bite you. When that occurs you're taxed at your standard income tax rate. There's no special tax savings on ordinary dividends.

But if you hold onto your stock long enough, it's classified as a qualified dividend and you don't pay income taxes. Rather, you pay capital gains taxes. These taxes are almost always at a rate lower than your income tax rate.

Putting on my thick glasses for a second here:

You pay no capital gains taxes up to the first $39,375 of your taxable income. None. As low as that sounds, with tax advantages, depreciation and other deductions, some years you may find yourself at that taxable income level (I help you get there in future chapters).

If your income is above $39,375 (up to $434,550), you only pay 15% in capital gains taxes. Whereas if you're earning that same level of income from an employer, you're taxed as high as 37%. Regardless of the income bracket you're in above that, the maximum you pay in capital gains tax is 20%. You see why the rich love stocks; less money leaves their pockets.

For a dividend of a stock to be "qualified," you must own the shares from the publicly traded company for at least 60 days during a 121-day period, starting 60 days prior to a company's ex-dividend date, which is the last date you can own shares and be entitled to the dividend.

Removing the thick glasses now. Eyes hurt.

This is all just the technical way of saying that you can't buy a stock before the company issues a dividend, collect that gift all shareholders have patiently waited for, and then sell and expect to have the same financial benefits as long term holders. If you try to time those dividend payouts, they're going to be classified as ordinary dividends and you'll be taxed at regular income tax rates.

In other words, you can't cut in line.

If you want to minimize your risk as much as possible and don't feel comfortable selecting individual stocks, you can invest in a mutual fund or ETF (exchange traded fund) of dividend stocks. This is where I mostly reside.

I'm partial to Vanguard, which created the world's first index mutual funds. They have an ETF called Vanguard Dividend Appreciation ETF. Its main goal is to track the performance of companies that increase their dividends year over year. Bingo.

In 2020 some of their largest holdings were Procter & Gamble, Johnson

& Johnson, and McDonald's - all companies with short-lived consumables, and thus dividends for you. You get exposure and diversification across all of these necessary, household goods. I suppose "necessary" is debatable. McFlurry ice cream? Really?

Diversification may be prudent. It is time honored advice. You are trusting professional managers to research and select the best stocks for you, so you don't have to. The homework is done for you.

But, contrary to popular opinion, diversification works both ways. Not only does it blunt losses by combining winning stocks, it dampens big wins by combining losing stocks - that's the part traditional money managers don't mention.

If you're confident and have done your research, go for a stock that checks off the boxes. Just don't go for a stock because it's a water-cooler stock. Usually, by the time a stock has made it to the water-cooler, it's too expensive. You want cheap stocks. And no one talks about cheap socks. When's the last time your friends talked about Walgreens stock to you? I rest my case.

Also, never invest more than you can afford to lose. That's called euphoria. It's what Ex-Fed Chairman Alan Greenspan called "irrational exuberance" during the late 1990s when internet stocks were about to go bust.

The Robinhood app is free (no brokerage fees), probably the easiest, and most simple for buying single stocks. And you can now buy them fractionally for as little as $1 of any company you want to invest in. This link (http://terencemichael.com/robinhood.html) will give you and me each one free stock. But there are others apps like Acorns, Stash, E*Trade, and TD Ameritrade. All solid apps that I've used in the past.

Speaking of TD Ameritrade (Toronto-Dominion Bank), even though they don't meet the criteria of having rising dividend yields every single year, they have at least been shelling out dividends to shareholders consistently since 1857. That's "18"! That's quite a record.

If you don't need the income, you can elect to have your dividends reinvested into buying more shares of the company. So even though you're not getting immediate income, you're acquiring more and more shares the longer you hold and re-invest, similar to compounding interest (what Einstein called the 8th wonder of the world).

But the purpose of this book is immediate, passive income, so, with that mandate, take the income if you want it, but keep your stocks long-term. You wouldn't likely sell that apartment building when you have tenants who renew despite annual rent increases. Keep collecting rent from Wall Street. Buy stocks that produce dividends.

7

Collect Mortgage Payments

*"You can use an eraser on the drafting table
or a sledgehammer on the construction site."*

- Frank Lloyd Wright

The majority of borrowers who need mortgages aren't typical nine to fivers with 10-year jobs at the same 6th floor cubicle with the same annoying boss who takes credit for the same things every time. Many need *private*, short-term mortgages of just 6-24 months.

Homeowners want to improve their house. They're ready for a remodeled kitchen or want to add a room for a growing family. Builders or developers may want a fixer-upper they can demolish, renovate, and turn into a rental or a flip for profit. And some people just need to consolidate their high credit card debt or take out cash for a 21-day trip around the world on a floating buffet.

These bridge loans provide a mechanism for borrowers to move swiftly outside traditional banking's laborious and paper-heavy loan process. Retail banks' underwriting standards are too restrictive for speculators or neglected properties.

Once these borrowers gain breathing room with the private loan, they can stabilize the property and later shop around for a cheaper, boilerplate loan to relax into for the long term.

Another example is the all-cash offer, which is usually just a private or "hard money" loan. If you've been house hunting, you know how aggressive it can become when prices are rising. Sellers may only accept over-ask or all-cash offers. And buyers have FOMO (Fear Of Missing Out). But who has that kind of cash to buy a house outright without a loan? Where do these filthy rich people come from?

Here's the truth: They aren't filthy rich. Most of those borrowers don't *really* have the entire house's list price sitting in a sparkly pile of cash. It's actually a hard-money loan. Stop beating yourself up. By quickly obtaining a short-term mortgage, borrowers receive the "cash" to close escrow. So the new cash becomes that bridge to get into the house; yet it is just another boring loan wearing cash's sexy clothing.

In any of these scenarios, you can become the holder of those bridge loans. You can be the bank. But you don't have to be the entire branch. You can fractionally join other "bankers" just like you, clubbing together to form the whole mortgage. This is accomplished with the click of a button, and in some cases for as cheap as two craft cocktails in frosty copper mugs.

You have all of the benefits, legal rights, remedies, and powers a bank does. You own the 1st lien that is publicly recorded on the property. You collect monthly mortgage payments of principal and interest. And you can foreclose if a payment plan or extension can't be worked out with the borrower.

That's the confidence with mortgage financing. You have the most valuable collateral in the world - property. As Mark Twain said, "They aren't making any more land." It's universal, transferable, and will forever be desirable, at least until we colonize space. Apparently there's a lot of room up there, which is probably why it's conveniently called "space."

Rather than the worthless collateral from my failed Craigslist days, a recorded, county lien on the borrower's house severely limits a borrower's choices if they default. In the event of nonpayment, they risk losing the house. You take it. You sell it. You get your money back *plus* whatever equity is still in the house.

Furthermore, these are senior-position liens only. Even if the borrower obtains other loans or lines of credit, they can only be recorded in 2nd or later position. A Lowe's Home Improvement card or HELOC (Home Equity line of Credit) would come after this 1st mortgage. So during a bankruptcy proceeding, the bank holding the HELOC and Lowe's would have to get in line behind you. They only get paid if you, the holder of the 1st lien, are first paid off in full. No shortcuts.

This protects your equity and gives you assurance. Only the IRS, with its authority to collect property taxes, supersedes lienholders.

The bottom line is motivation. No one wants to lose their house. There's no upside. No one wants to lose all the equity they've built up over time, which likely began with their original down payment.

If borrowers default, they lose two valuable assets - the value of the house upon sale as well as the physical shelter itself. There's seldom a scenario where anyone is trying to game a bridge-loan with the intention of foreclosing. The cards are stacked in the lender's favor, giving him a royal flush.

Here's where everything you just read gets even better: this is all crowdsourced online. Much like the P2P sites in chapter 3, you don't have to do any of the labor. Platforms do it for you and take a small percentage (1-1.5%) of the deal, which they charge the borrower, not you.

You need not stress or supervise any of the mechanics of these loans. The clubhouse where you and the other bankers have congregated is designed for sinking into leather chairs and enjoying a good read. The clubhouse does everything and then brings you profits on a Queen Anne serving tray.

These crowdfunding sites thrive at the intersection between tech and real estate. The venture capitalists and executives behind them are both real estate veterans and Silicon valley innovators. Together they act as trusted deputies for lenders and borrowers.

The sites vet the borrowers, run credit scores, background checks, conduct appraisals, verify income, confirm debt, check assets, etc. These bridge platforms even conduct the mundane necessary work in person with inspectors and local real estate professionals to examine every deal. They utilize the same lens as retail banks, but do it with expediency and efficiency.

And for that, they charge borrowers much higher interest rates.

Technically, some of these lending platforms are already underwriting and issuing mortgages before you invest. But they need investors to replenish their capital pool to turn around and sign the next set of borrowers to add deal-flow for investors (you).

You want to earn interest as soon as possible. This is why the platforms have to be out in front to close deals so you can hit the ground running by the time you get involved. They cook the pie and then offer you ready-to-eat slices.

Let's start with GroundFloor, since anyone can participate for as little as $25 per deal. Here's a link: http://terencemichael.com/groundfloor.html.

The interest rates at GroundFloor can run from 6-7% on the low end to over 15% on the high end. Rates adjust per the property's equity, length of loan, and borrower's creditworthiness, just like P2P deals.

I've had 76 mortgages pay off here, all of them with at least 9.5% annual rates; many are well over 14%. Most properties tend to be simple, single-family homes on the east coast - a lot of volume from Georgia and North Carolina. Only 1 has gone into default.

Another platform is PeerStreet (http://terencemichael.com/peerstreet.html). The drawback of PeerStreet is that the minimum investment is $1,000 for any one property. But it's my favorite.

At PeerStreet, I've had 634 loans pay off. Currently, 51 additional loans are still active and paying, and 3 have gone into default. Even with the defaults, I'm averaging over 8%. Most newer loans at the moment are paying over 10% due to the inflated economy and potential housing price decreases.

And remember, defaults do not equate to a loss of money. In almost all cases, it simply delays the return of your principal. You still own the 1st position lien. You have that collateral. If need be, you activate that lien to take the borrower all the way to foreclosure when other payback options can't be achieved.

Deployment of initial funds, depending on how much you're starting with can take some time. Similar to the P2P lending sites in chapter 3, once you get fully invested with enough volume, these become cash waterfalls. Deals can complete every week or day.

The other drawback of PeerStreet (not so with GroundFloor) is that you must be an "accredited investor." But don't let that hinder your journey.

Accreditation will change in the future, so I would familiarize yourself with PeerStreet. The SEC is quickly updating rules for online investing requirements, so I'm confident this restriction will soon loosen, especially post COVID-19. But at the moment it's a *soft* requirement.

I say "soft" because some of the sites in this accreditation space handle the qualifications on the honor system. They can only approve or decline you based on what *you tell them*. Although I'm not encouraging you to mislead, it's not a difficult process to become accredited if you so wish.

To be an accredited investor you don't need to obtain a license or take a course. Accreditation is simply a snapshot of your wealth.

If you're fortunate enough to have a net worth of $1 million or more excluding the value of your principal residence, then you qualify as an accredited investor. Done. Nothing else to do, other than congratulate yourself for making the sacrifices to get here.

Net worth is calculated by taking all of your assets, bank statements, stocks, retirement accounts, artwork, whatever you have of value and deducting your liabilities such as mortgages and student loans.

I have friends and clients who were positive they wouldn't qualify for accreditation. Not even close. But when we walked through the process, many discovered they did. Some hold title as part of a family trust. Some are partners in a business with net worth. Some own other valuable assets like an insurance policy, an annuity, antique cars, or ownership in a patent.

If that doesn't work, the other method is your current income over the last two years. If you can show that you made at least $200,000 each of the last two years, and can state that you have a "reasonable expectation" for that to continue into the near future, you are accredited. If you are married, this figure is $300,000 combined for the two of you.

In either case, net worth or income qualify you to be an accredited investor. You don't need to meet both (and most can't).

There is a 3rd way: Your broker or CPA can examine your situation and write a one-paragraph letter on her letterhead stating that you are an accredited investor. Whether you really are or not, I'll leave that up to you and your CPA.

Stepping on my soapbox for a minute, here's my take:

Investors are adults. They realize risk comes with any investment. Yet it's severely limited when it's over-collateralized. So why limit people based on their income or assets from enjoying the benefits that only the rich have access to?

I find it peculiar that anyone can spend $1,000 on lottery scratch-offs from the corner donut shop without any qualifications whatsoever. But you can't invest that same amount of money in a safe mortgage-backed asset with effectively no risk of principal return? Don't even get me started on the odds difference in these two scenarios.

If you're willing to accept responsibility for an investment, then criteria met. That's my philosophy, and I suspect one many others share as well. So again, read into it what you must, but you have to be accredited for PeerStreet. If not, GroundFloor has got you covered. And really, they're effectively the same.

Stepping off my soapbox.

The SEC already took a leap forward in this financing-reserved-for-the-rich area by allowing crowdsourced real estate investing in the first place. The *Jumpstart Our Business Startups Act* (JOBS act) of 2012 allowed investors to seek money online. In 2016 this was updated to include crowdfunding.

This is precisely what I needed in order to promote my employees from LendingClub and Prosper. And it's added a steady stream of income for me, as well as hundreds of thousands of people.

Here are the nuts and bolts:

If you decide to invest $1,000 of a house in Florida seeking a $200,000 mortgage, you become a 0.5% owner of that mortgage.

$1,000 investment / $200,000 mortgage = 0.5% mortgage share

You receive 0.5% of all monthly payments on this mortgage.

Let's suppose this mortgage is paying an interest-only 9% for a 12-month term (typical).

.09 interest rate x $200,000 mortgage = $18,000 per year

$18,000 per year / 12 months = $1,500 a month interest

That comes to $1,500 a month in interest payments received by the investor pool. Since you took 0.5% of the entire pool, you get 0.5% of the $1,500 every month, or $90 for the term of the loan, plus your $1,000 principal at expiration.

$1,500 a month interest x 0.5% mortgage share = $7.5 per month

$7.5 x 12 months = $90 total interest

$1,000 principle + $90 interest = $1,090 returned to you over 12 months.

Now extrapolate this to numerous deals and you're making reasonable side income. Meanwhile, you're contemplating other deals to diversify into.

You can ladder these deals such that once you have enough of them going, you always have prior ones coming due. So what is otherwise an illiquid investment in the short-term becomes liquid via recurring due dates.

I've been with these real estate debt-financing platforms for over 5 years now. I get almost daily emails of loans coming due since I'm investing in new ones almost every day. Some days I've made $47. Other days I've made over $5,000. It just depends on the size of the loans and volume of the ones coming due on that day. Oftentimes I simply let the money invest in more deals. But other times I move it upstream for even higher rates, as outlined in subsequent chapters.

Here is my criteria for selecting the best deals:

1. LTV

Loan-To-Value is perhaps the most important of all ratios to look at. As you know from prior chapters, this is a standard qualifier across almost all types of lending from Peer-to-Peer to Stablecoins. It's the most important ratio for bankers, so you can't avoid seeing it surface everywhere you look with your new banker's spectacles.

Should a borrower default, you want to know there is enough padding to cover foreclosure expenses, attorneys fees, agency commissions, as well as your principal and interest. You want to confirm that the collateral is worth a fair amount more than the actual loan.

I rarely agree to any of these mortgage deals with an LTV over 75%. So if a house seeking a bridge loan is appraised with its current value at $1,000,000 and the borrower is seeking a loan of $800,000, that's an 80% LTV.

$800,000 mortgage / $1,000,000 value = 80% LTV

If they default on an $800,000 mortgage, you obtain the rights to a $1,000,000 house. Doesn't sound bad with $200,000 in equity.

But the house may need to be repaired or maintained, the market may have shifted downward recently, and the foreclosure process is inefficient and expensive. It takes sometimes months, with possibly an eviction, courthouse negotiations, potential borrower bankruptcy, realtor swaps, staging, open houses, escrow fallouts, etc.

The courts do everything possible to allow the borrower to remedy the debt, even up until the last minute on courthouse steps with a dramatic game show level reveal. So delays are to be expected.

With that said, you are certainly protected with an equity buffer. But personally I want even more protection should that pillow lose some of its stuffing overnight.

Ideally, I like to see deals at 70% LTV or lower. The interest rate I earn might be slightly less, but I accept that reduction in order to protect my neck with a fluffy pillow. I want the borrower to be set up for success. It helps both of us sleep well at night and wake up in perfect alignment.

Be cognizant of ARV, or After-Repair-Value. Many of these crowdsourced real estate investing sites, like GroundFloor, use ARV instead of LTV (PeerStreet uses the more conservative LTV). That in itself isn't a bad thing. But the difference is imperative in your evaluation.

The property is undergoing more significant renovations if there's an ARV, so the "value" of the house is in its *planned future*, not its current state. So it can be dangerous to mistake ARV as LTV. It's that pesky "R" that you have to observe.

Sticking with the same example above, if that house seeking an $800,000 mortgage has an ARV of 80%, it means that the $800,000 you lend to the borrower is against a house valued at $1,000,000 in the future, *after repairs*. That $1,000,000 valuation is a forecast of what the house might be worth after major renovations (or an entire build) are completed. Not as appraised today.

Maybe the current value of the house is closer to $900,000 than $1,000,000. It's the repairs and improvements that are giving it a projected appraisal of $1,000,000. In this case, the *current* LTV is actually 88%.

$800,000 mortgage / $900,000 value = 88% LTV

That's cutting it close when you add in the fees and repairs for resale. And the real estate market would need only dip 10% and you're suddenly at 98% LTV - effectively no collateral. Real estate commissions alone will gut 5-6%. Now you're looking at an upside down LTV. It's more like VTL (Venture-To-Lose).

I invest in ARVs in the 60% or less range for these reasons. While writing this paragraph, I checked GroundFloor and found six deals in the 43-58% ARV range. I took action on all of them at $250 a piece. Although the minimums at GroundFloor are as low as $25, I've discovered I do no better or worse deploying $250. And each one saves me nine other clicks for the same amount of money.

Here's an example of a 60% ARV deal:

A $400,000 appraised house is seeking a $300,000 mortgage to add a 2nd floor to increase the livable space. With that added square footage, the appraiser estimates the house will be worth $500,000 in 12 months time.

As you can see, the ARV is 60%.

$300,000 mortgage / $500,000 after repair value = 0.60

But the true LTV is actually much higher at 75%.

$300,000 mortgage / $400,000 value = .75

2. Credit Score

The 2nd most important factor for me is the credit score. I'll contradict what I said earlier and say that occasionally I'll take an 80% LTV or 70% ARV (higher than my comfortable ceilings) if the borrower has an abnormally high credit score like 800+. You can't reach credit scores in the 800s without stellar debt-loads and responsible paybacks.

Even though a 680-700 credit score represents a "good" borrower, they either have some blemishes or they're carrying too much debt elsewhere, perhaps on credit cards.

I have clients in my mortgage business who have sub-700 scores. They have high income levels, work steady jobs, and have significant assets. But their debt is irresponsibly managed through credit card swaps, high balances, or by simply missing a payment here or there. All of those factors make lenders nervous.

Quick side note on credit cards: never carry a balance greater than 30% of the available credit on *each* credit card you own. That is the single best way to keep your credit scores high. This shows you can manage your available credit without pushing it to the edge. This is also a great hack to exercise at least 30 days before buying a house to boost your scores.

One more quick side note on credit cards: If you shop at Amazon, stop what you are doing right now and get the Amazon Prime Rewards Visa Signature Card. Although I'm not in favor of credit cards, this card is a money-saving hack. It's issued and linked to your online Amazon account, so everything - literally everything you buy on Amazon - gives you 5% cash back. There is nothing you need to do other than have that card be your linked payment. To seal the deal, select the option where you don't even get a card. You don't need it. You don't want it. Just have it sit there in Amazon's money-printing vault to spit out 5% cash back every time you buy anything on Amazon.

Commercial break over.

The credit bureaus (Experian, Equifax, TransUnion) all utilize similar scoring systems such that you don't have to dig through a borrower's debt and credit history. The score from any of those bureaus is a valuable indicator.

While writing this paragraph, I just flipped over to PeerStreet and found two deals with credit scores at 765 and 810 with LTVs of 75%. That LTV is 5% higher than I prefer, but with those credit scores, I'm taking them. $1,000 a piece. And the interest on each is over 11%.

3. Run-of-the-Mill

The 3rd factor I use in these types of loans is a bit of common sense. I simply flip through the photos and ask myself, "Is this a house Jack Jones and

Sarah Smith would want to buy and live in?" If we have to foreclose on the borrower and put it up for sale to liquidate it, are we going to have trouble selling it?

I can view on Google if it's across from a school. Pass. I can see from the photos if it's over-built for the neighborhood. Pass. I can see if the neighbors' yards resemble the junkyard from *Making A Murderer*. Pass. Common sense.

I learned all these the hard way. I've done over 800 of these loans over the years (other platforms below). Not flexing, but want to impress upon you how automatic and accessible these platforms can be. With that level of activity, I'm also guilty of mindlessly clicking around without paying attention. These platforms make it that easy to invest while sitting at a red light or evading a boring conversation from a talkative neighbor obsessed with the weather (I live in L.A. Yeah, it's nice out. I get it. Thanks for the breaking news).

My first default was a massive $2.6M house in Palm Springs. The place was on a hill, had a gorgeous view and was as luxurious as they get. I thought, okay how can I lose? This is amazing. Beautiful house. Beautiful view. The LTV was higher at 80%. Strike 1. And I forgot to look at the credit, which takes all of two seconds. Strike 2. But I was in awe of the house. I wanted the house myself!

I plunked down $2,000 for a 9% return as part of the investor group so that the borrower could finish his remodel and put the house on the market. Strike 3. You know what comes after that. This was on PeerStreet and I could have easily just taken the $1k minimum. But I was salivating with greed, influenced by too many Gordon Gekko memes.

It didn't turn out as planned. Four or five months into the 12-month loan the borrower stopped making payments and went silent. Long story short, the borrower got in over his head, gutted the house and decided for whatever reason to walk away, house half completed.

After some extensions, renegotiations, stop-and-starts, the house became ours (the investor pool) - all coordinated through PeerStreet. They negotiated with the borrower, filed for notice of default, argued numerous court hearings, hired attorneys, completed the unfinished rehab, hired realtors, fired realtors, rehired new realtors, went into escrow several times, and lowered the list price three times to eventually find the right buyer.

It was an arduous process. And one where I wasn't alone at the Santa Monica courthouse crossing my fingers the borrower wouldn't show up.

The biggest problem, and the lesson I learned, was that a $2.6M house, as beautiful as it is, has few buyers. Just how many people can afford a $2.6M vacation house? And of those that can afford that house, how many of them have to have this exact one, in this specific location, at the exact time of sale?

I now only invest in the average, run-of-the-mill house. I don't want the baller Miami mansion on the beach where music videos are shot. I also don't want the one bedroom condo adjacent the freeway, no matter how convenient realtors convince you it is. I just want a typical, suburban home-home (when you say it twice it makes it normal).

Remember those old sitcoms you grew up watching? Those homes. I want those homes that every dysfunctional sitcom family seemed to live in and learn life lessons like, "Don't play ball in the house."

In the end, I received something like $1,960 back. So I lost $40 on that mid-century house. But that was a win for me. And an inexpensive tax deductible $40 lesson that would have cost me three times that from a Udemy or Gumroad course. It also solidifies why I love these crowdfunding sites so much. This was one of the rare times I was involved in a default. And it was also a rare time I took the time to monitor the process. But I wanted to learn.

I'm sure many investors had no idea it even defaulted. Most just see their balance going up every day, looking at the aggregate and not the individual details of each deal. This is where I sit today with PeerStreet and GroundFloor. I rarely dive into the notices or details unless I have a client who has pinged me with questions. My time is better spent plowing ahead and managing where the profits go - back to the factory floor, or upstairs for other opportunities.

FundThatFlip is one such opportunity upstairs. It is for accredited investors (and those wanting to learn). The minimums are steep: $5,000. These minimums may be lower in the future, so don't exclude yourself if this isn't feasible today. But with that comes generous interest rates in the 10-14% range with very short turnaround times: 12 months max. Many are 4 to 6 months.

This is one of many places builders and developers get their funds when they find a bare piece of land and want to develop 8 townhomes to sell. It's where they apply when they have a major fixer or a complete tear-down. It's where they go when they want to convert a 6-unit apartment building into 6 individual condos. In other words, it's where they go to Fund. That. Flip.

FundThatFlip fully vets the developers, construction plans, blueprints, location's viability, etc. They also disburse the funds at various milestones that need to be met on schedule with proper inspections and permits. They keep the builders, architects, and contractors in check and make sure funds are being used for their intended purpose.

The main difference is the risk/reward ratio. In real estate, the further your initial investment from the finished product, the greater the risk. There are more things that can go wrong when there's a square piece of dirt than when there are 5 sparkly new condos 12 months later.

At FundThatFlip I've invested in 42 projects. 19 of them have fully paid off. 23 of them are still active and performing. And 3 are late and working on extensions or new refinances. Most of these projects reside in New Jersey, Philadelphia, and Brooklyn. I'm newer to FundThatFlip, so am not as seasoned there as at PeerStreet or GroundFloor, but I love the returns so far.

Like PeerStreet and GroundFloor, you have the same protections with 1st liens, appraisals, credit scores, borrower background and experience. You continue to collect automatically and passively.

The time spent is whatever level of scrutiny you want to conduct combing through the financials. Once you get the hang of it, it may take you all of two minutes to make a decision on a deal. Those two minutes on a 12-month $5,000 deal at 12% gives you $50 a month for the next year, and then the return of your $5,000.

Aside from the same circumstances we just covered, like LTV/ARV and credit, with FundThatFlip we additionally want to scrutinize the borrower's contribution ("skin in the game"). Builders and developers personally commit their own cash to the deal. I use this as a measurement of their confidence.

If, for example, the development project is a $4 million dollar dirt lot for 4 new homes (both purchase and construction budget), and the borrower is contributing say $75,000, I move on.

$75,000 is an amount of cash you wouldn't think a developer would walk away from. But It's less than 2% of the deal. If things go sour during construction, it will be easier for the builder to leave $75,000 on the table than repay a $4,000,0000 deal. I want to know that the developer has done everything possible to put every dime he has into the project. This tells me he believes in it enough to share in the outcome (as opposed to guaranteeing a paycheck for himself).

There's an additional advantage with these developer deals with respect to credit scores: many of them involve several partners, co-borrowers, and LLCs, all with their own credit scores and guarantees. They are typically teams of contractors, attorneys, and real estate brokers who all together *and separately* guarantee the loan. There is more than one debtor to chase if need be. Odds are one can't run as fast as the others.

I've seen dozens of deals on FundThatFlip where 3 or more of the borrowers all had 740+ scores. I can't click on those deals fast enough. Because even though you're investing $5,000 instead of PeerStreet's $1,000 or GroundFloor's $25, your investment is *less* at risk when factoring the double or triple backstops should foreclosure happen.

Plan for the worst, hope for the best. This adage will serve you well with these deals. It's a numbers game. It's a volume game. And it's one the banks no longer play alone. You're invited.

8

Don't Buy Your House

"Real estate cannot be lost or stolen,
nor can it be carried away.
Purchased with common sense,
it is about the safest investment in the world."

- Franklin D. Roosevelt

I love home ownership. I habitually promote the benefits, of which there are many. But when you do the math it may surprise you that it makes more sense to own *income property* than your principal residence.

In other words: don't buy the home you want to live in.

It's true you can mitigate the risks of buying your own home and make a decent profit on the property. Perhaps you've done it. I've done it. But it's also possible we were lucky.

People who make money with their own residences:

- may catch real estate cycles at the right time

- are experienced flippers or remodelers, so they can add sweat equity

- are willing to buy undervalued property and live in dust and debris

- are adventurous enough to live in submarkets that haven't improved much yet

- can commit to living in the home for a minimum of 10 years

- can afford the home's ancillary debt should they lose their job

- can take advantage of IRS Code 121

IRS Code 121 is one significant outlier when it comes to favoring the purchase of a home you live in. But timing needs to line up. If you're intrepid and time your moves properly, it can be exceptionally lucrative.

The U.S. government allows you to eliminate any taxes on the first $250,000 of profit ($500,000 if married) when you sell the home you live in, so long as, during the previous 5 years, you have occupied it an aggregate of 2 years. How else can you earn money and not pay taxes on it? This is equivalent to earning another 30% or so saving federal and state taxes.

In simple numbers: Buy a house for $300,000. Live in it. Sell it for $600,000 for a $300,000 profit. That's a capital gain on which you must normally pay taxes, just like dividends in chapter 6.

But the IRS allows a single person to take that first $250,000 and put it in their pocket. You're only taxed on the remaining $50,000. And that's without factoring in commissions and cost basis, which likely wipes out most of that $50,000 anyway.

It's really tough to beat this offering. However, the longer you live in your house, which is often necessary to accommodate real estate cycles and personal convenience, the less this rule benefits you. The opportunity cost of your home ownership (the down payment and all accompanying costs) grows each day beyond the two-year period. The benefit only exists if you exercise it.

When I was younger and didn't mind living among jagged, broken tile, in a sketchy neighborhood with Bondo-patched cars on cinder blocks, and showering at LA Fitness when the plumbing didn't exist, I leveraged this rule almost every 2 years to achieve tax-free income (you can re-activate this benefit every 2 years). I thought I was Einstein in boots and overalls.

In hindsight, it was a lot of work. What I attributed to my *Property Brothers* skills may have been fortunate timing. Maybe there would have been a profitable sale in spite of my mosaic kitchen countertops and interior windows. And how ideal would this operation be for someone with kids and school districts to consider?

If you're good with all of those, odds are you won't *lose* any money with home-ownership.

But what's the definition of "lose?" Homeowners think if they sell a house for more than they paid, they haven't lost. But they have failed to calculate the hidden costs of that home.

I've spoken with the CEO/Founders of Redfin, HomeAdvisor, The Corcoran Group, ERA Realty, TheAgency, etc. Unanimously, they agree that home ownership is probably the best investment anyone can make over the long term. But rarely do people know what their long-term plans are. So it's the short-term that often takes over any long-term plans.

I've also interviewed popular HGTV personalities/flippers/developers like Anthony Carrino and Matt Blashaw. They've reminded me that people lose their shirts tying emotion to investment. It's very difficult to separate the two when it's your own home. They also agree that unless you're moving a flip quickly, like within 3 to 4 months, you lose the value of the flip due to recurring costs and long-term maintenance.

When I do the math, I would have made *more* money in the long run had I taken that identical financial buying power and purchased out-of-state income property. That leverage would be the aggregate of all of my cash down payments for all the house purchases, closing costs, monthly mortgages, annual property taxes, and costs to improve, maintain, repair, landscape and insure.

All of those costs over the years put into buy-and-hold properties with the same dollar for dollar leveraging with mortgages would have eventually given me the same profit about 10 years later. Then, beyond the 10 years, it would be bonus money for life.

So it would have taken longer to achieve the same results, but today I would still have all of those income properties with higher rents, most likely double if not triple appreciation, and more write-offs than I would know what to do with. Actually, I know exactly what to do with them.

That's my opportunity cost - the potential prospect and impact that specific amount of home-buying money could have elsewhere. Economists say that's the true cost of anything.

Of course, I was fortunate to make large chunks of money when I sold my residences. Very grateful. Those gave me financial confidence early on. But they certainly weren't guaranteed. And they were the furthest from passive income you can imagine.

I've never sweat more, been more stressed, and physically worked so hard as I did rehabbing houses. Who knows if there won't be some long-term effects of scraping asbestos ceilings or pulling out installation from 1927 homes? I try not to think about it.

Again, I might have just caught the real estate wave in the right direction long enough to confirm my bias for sweat equity and DIY YouTube videos.

Let's be honest: we like the story of owning a home. We feel it bolsters our identity. We say, "I am the type of person who *owns*, not rent. I have a level of success such that I can buy my own home. I'm an adult. I'm successful."

This is what we telegraph to the world to impress others - often people we don't really care about, and who don't care about us. This is an unfortunate figment of our imagination. It's a scorecard for a dumb game that puts people into financial stress. Other people don't care if you rent or own. They're worried about their own finances. And if they *are* impressed, how expensive is that impression for you?

What I find impressive is someone who is happy and at peace. That takes deliberate dedication to get there with financial freedom. I covet someone's ability to be happy and debt free no matter whether their house is owned by a landlord or the bank.

And that's just it.

When you own, you still have a landlord. You still have to pay rent. It's called the bank and they collect a monthly mortgage. Just like renting, you still put down a security deposit, but it's a huge percentage (maybe all) of your savings rather than one month's rent. Add to that: property taxes, monthly maintenance, quarterly repairs, weekly landscaping, homeowners insurance, and liability insurance - all things a landlord covers if you simply rent.

Banks love this landlord/tenant relationship. They've carefully developed and helped rebrand this as "home ownership." They understand just how important this virtue and social signaling is for most people.

Financial institutions will help you achieve your dreams. You'll thank them profusely. But they hold the lien. You are indebted to them. And if you don't pay your rent on time, they'll take *their* house back from you.

Much of this stems from post WWII slogans in the 1940s promoted by real estate companies who needed to sell homes quickly to accommodate growing families due to "war babies" (baby boomers). "The American Dream" was nothing more than clever advertising copy for real estate developers.

The government supports this. It helps the economy. When families buy homes, they prompt construction, design, decoration, and dozens of other home services and products for businesses.

Ownership creates pride and beautifies neighborhoods, which raises the value of counties, which raises property taxes, and hopefully keeps people employed and off assistance programs.

70% of all mortgages are insured or purchased by the government in the form of Fannie or Freddie Mac loans. When the government guarantees these loans, it allows banks to immediately offload their mortgages and go underwrite new ones, continuing to collect fees for processing and servicing the loans.

With the government's support as a guaranteed buyer for every lender, easy mortgages generate easy debt for every family. Debt keeps families working for a paycheck, paying their taxes, consuming products and services, which in turn cultivates the economy's GDP (gross domestic product).

And the government allows LTV ratios of as high as 96.5%! So home buyers starting out with only 3.5% equity in a house are susceptible to mild swings, leaving them at times with no equity.

The term "mortgage" itself is somewhat ominous. "Mort" literally means "death," as in mortician or mortuary. And "gage" is a glove thrown to the ground to start a quarrel or fight, as in "engage" (yet couples still get engaged).

In England, land was only granted to a commoner from the Lords (land *lord*), if they signed a "death engagement," i.e. a mort-gage. You can see why the narrative was reshaped from engaging in death into The American Dream; has a slightly better ring to it.

I don't view any of this with pessimism. I love real estate and the birdshot effect it creates for the economy as a whole. I think home ownership and the leverage of mortgages is one of the best financial moves anyone can make.

What I take issue with is the fantasy that we need to stretch our finances for the single largest investment we will ever make *because* it is The American Dream. The American Dream involves you buying the home for you, not you buying a home for someone else. That's not what we're taught to dream. It's much easier to sell a dream kitchen than it is freedom. Yet which would you prefer?

Actually, you can have both.

The white picket fence, the perfectly manicured lawn, the BBQ station in the back, the high-ceilings and open space kitchen - you can have this idyllic utopia for yourself. But the revelation is if you rent this for yourself rather than buy it, it saves you money and mental space.

When you buy a home to live in, you buy a situation with less flexibility than if you rent that same house. You now sacrifice the freedom of renting for much higher housing expenses.

You can't pick-up and move where you want, when you want, as often as you want. The plasticity of renting allows you to be fluid. Go find the home you want and get the exact yard you want. Tenants may have the ultimate negotiating power as there can be endless choices. Not true as a home buyer.

Homeowners are often jealous of renter immunity. Homeowners can be stuck with bad neighbors, a barking dog, noisy street, distance from a job change, kids switching schools, or some other unforeseen incurable factor like installation of a new 5G cell phone tower they didn't notice when buying the perfectly staged home.

Part of the problem is that a home buyer's strategy is contingent on that one event taking place at some point in the future to make them financially whole: the sale. This one event is critical to make everything worthwhile over the next 3, 5, 10 or more years of expense.

What's the aggregate of all of those expenses during the duration of home ownership? If put to paper, it would scare most homeowners to learn how much "rent" they actually paid for that house.

You have to get the timing right when you sell. And your lifestyle has to allow for it. If this aligns perfectly, you "win" with a sale making you whole.

But where are you moving next?

Most people who sell their primary residences have to buy another house. They end up using all of the profit from the prior house for the next one. Statistics show that most of the time the next one has more square footage, more rooms, more land, more furniture, more storage, more property taxes, and more debt. More.

Downsizing feels like a loss. And so it often comes involuntarily once there *is* a loss.

Somehow it makes more sense that we write checks to a bank rather than a landlord. But it's the costly story we continue to perpetuate.

The real issue is that this relationship of home and investment is a marriage of inconvenience. We mesh the largest investment of our lifetime with a place to sleep, eat, and spend time with our family.

Just ask the millions of people who bought homes and lost fortunes, went bankrupt, and are still in debt from the 2008-2009 housing crisis. Ask them if in hindsight they would have still made those home purchases if they were given a mulligan.

How many income-generating rental properties would the housing crisis owners have had for the same amount of money they invested and lost? How much income would they have made (and would still be making today) with long-term holds?

It doesn't matter where the economy is, or if Wall Street is up or down, people need a place to live. It's why owning income properties is one of the greatest wealth builders of all time.

Another argument I hear from homeowners is that they can finally do whatever they want to the place. They want more room for the kids. They want to paint walls, put in wood flooring, build bookshelves, or finally get those smart appliances that tell you when you're out of eggs or need to buy more detergent. When they rent, they are stuck with the owner's choices.

This is another misconception that helps justify the story of home ownership. Having been a renter numerous times, and now being a landlord of over 20 income properties, I can tell you just how wrong this perception is.

The only thing stopping a tenant from doing anything they want is the security deposit. That's what the security deposit is for - to compensate for any "unacceptable" changes/damages to the property.

Outside of that, a tenant lives there. They are allowed to *live*. It's their place. It's not a hotel that in 2 days needs to continue the company's cookie-cutter corporate branding for the next set of guests.

I have rented apartments and ripped out old carpet and appliances, and put in new sink faucets. Not only was my landlord excited that I improved and raised the value of his place, he actually gave me 3 months' rent free once he saw what I did.

I have clients who have done this too, more successfully than I. They've gotten their landlord to pay for all materials, once he was presented with a plan. Materials are cheap. Labor is expensive. It's a win-win for the landlord. He gets free upgrades and can raise the rent when the renter moves out.

If your landlord doesn't like your alterations because you inherited your design taste from binging *Hoarders* TV episodes, he will keep your security deposit. Fine. What's the loss of your security deposit? 1 month's, 2 month's rent max? How does that compare to the loss of equity in the home you had to buy just so you could tailor it to you and compete with your neighbors in the process? A security deposit is a small form of insurance when you rent.

If a landlord won't budge and says "No" to everything, you have even more leverage: move. Go rent the house you want. It exists. And the fact is, even homeowners get tired of their upgrades and design. What was shiny and new 5 years ago that you paid $100,000 to upgrade becomes dated.

Just within the last 10 years we've seen a movement from classical dark woods and colors to clean grays and farm sinks to then rustic and reclaimed open space to boho desert whites and florals. Just 5 years ago, you found the search term "stainless steel" appliances in every home description. Now no one cares. They want white, red, or black appliances. That permanent space is sometimes temporary.

I make the argument for renting your own home and buying income property for three main reasons:

1. The 1% Rule

This says you shouldn't own a home if you can't get a minimum of 1% of the value of the home in monthly rent. Whether you are buying a home to live in or as income property makes no difference. You still want to achieve this 1% rule if you are purchasing. Hold onto that thought.

2. Expenses are deductible

You can't deduct expenses for the home you live in, but you can for the home you rent to others. Many people get this wrong. All those repairs and maintenance costs have zero benefit financially. Those are lost forever, unless you own the home *as a rental*. When it's a rental, it's a business. And you can deduct business expenses. Hold onto this thought as well.

3. The 27.5 Rule

You can't depreciate the home you live in, but can the home you rent to others. This is the single best tax benefit of owning an income rental property. It's a real expense with an artificial payment. Pay attention to this rule as it will influence the next two chapters.

Let's now explore each of these three factors in detail.

The 1% rule states that if you can rent a property *monthly* for 1% of its total asking price, it's worth buying.

An $850,000 house that can only collect $3,000 a month, isn't a house I would buy.

$3,000 a month rent / $850,000 value = .3%

That house is getting less than 1/3rd what it should to meet this rule.

To achieve the 1% rule, it would need to get $8,500 a month in rent.

$8,500 a month in rent / $850,000 value = 1%.

All other considerations aside, you're buying something that has more economic value (rent) than the sticker-price value (purchase).

Rental rates in a property's neighborhood is an efficient barometer for the value of living there. Run this test with where you live right now, whether you rent or own. It will reveal if your house would be worth buying today. Go to Redfin or Zillow and find your address. Take the estimate of its value today and multiply that by .01 (1%).

A $1M house would have to generate $10,000 a month in rent to reach that 1% threshold. That is impossible where I live in Los Angeles. A $10,000 a month rental would come from a property with a value north of $2.5M.

What this tells me is that it's smarter to rent in L.A. than buy. Monthly rental rates in Los Angeles are closer to 0.4% or less of a property's value. That makes it smart for renters, less smart for owners.

My personal residence would sell today for $1.4M. But I could never rent it out today for $14,000 per month. That's the 1% floor I would need to achieve the baseline. I could maybe get $6,500 a month on an extremely good day, which is 0.4%. Not 1%.

It's one reason I'm seeing more and more families move into my neighborhood as renters, not owners. It's more affordable to rent than buy (and smarter, in this case).

The 1% rule is effectively the mathematical confirmation of affordability.

Let's head over to some areas in Tennessee, Oklahoma, Indiana, Ohio, and Michigan. Today I can buy a $35,000 rental house (the entire house) and get $700 a month in rent in any one of these states.

That rent level doubles the 1% rule.

$700 a month rent / $35,000 home value = 2%

The rent ratio is skewed so far in my favor as an owner that I can capture 2-fold this rent ratio rule on the first day.

What if you bought nothing but 2% properties? The person who would pay $1.4M for my house today would, on average, put 20% cash down and obtain an 80% mortgage.

$280,000 down + $1,120,000 mortgage = $1.4M

You could take that same purchasing capability and buy 40 $35,000 houses.

40 houses x $35,000 average price = $1.4M

Those 40 houses at $700 monthly rent is $28,000 a month, or 2%.

So someone would be better off collecting this $28,000 a month by owning multiple income properties, and renting a place like mine for $6,500 a month, pocketing $21,500 a month in profit (the difference).

In other words, buy the $1.4M worth of income properties that meet the 2% rule and turn around and rent the $1.4M house you want to live in. Pocket the difference.

You'd spend the same amount of down payment as you would with your own residence and acquire the same amount of debt. Identical. You're just shifting the investment upstream, elsewhere, where the RTV (Rent-To-Value) rate is significantly higher.

I'm leaving out expenses for easy math. But you'll see why below, as those expenses come with benefits.

These deals are all over the nation but require time to search and find them. That's why I love the real estate platform, Roofstock (link: http://terencemichael.com/roofstock.html)

Roofstock investigates and secures performing rental income properties and lists them on their site for purchase. Unlike other crowdsourcing sites, you aren't investing or buying fractionally. You are legally buying the entire house. All of it.

Except, it's very different.

Roofstock does the homework for you that no brick and mortar agency will provide. They seek and list properties that are essentially turn-key. The listings have tenant-verified leases, property management companies, insurance, and even mortgages, all ready to go when you buy.

They take the typical obstacles most buyers face when trying to buy an income property and solve them upfront. They then hand them to you in a nifty little box on your web browser.

There's even a 30-day money-back guarantee. Nowhere else in real estate does this kind of buyer protection exist. But Roofstock is so confident in their analysis and due diligence that they can afford this guarantee.

Furthermore, with Roofstock's search filters, you can separate out properties based on preference such as: geography, price, cap rates, appreciation, school districts, neighborhood appeal, and… *even the 1% rule*.

Of course, you don't have to purchase these as rentals. But Roofstock has curated their inventory for income property optimization.

Some homes have better appreciation potential. Some are Section 8 housing where you get guaranteed checks from the government. Some are duplexes. Many are relatively inexpensive. All are for sale. And anyone can make an offer.

Roofstock is in over 70 markets and closes over 500 transactions a month. I've never seen so much user-friendly information on income property in one place. Aside from walking the property personally, Roofstock has covered everything else you could think of.

I've interviewed the CEO and Founder of Roofstock, Gary Beasley. He said that Roofstock has the purchasing power to basically buy up every single house that ever comes on the market. They have advanced algorithms and data scientists who comb every deal. But they don't want every home. They only want the homes that make financial sense for investors.

Roofstock deliberately buys houses that have positive cash flow on day one, which is rare for income investors. Most investors have to invest significant capital and wait at least 18 months to 2 years before starting to turn the corner on their debt load.

The downside is Roofstock may not be in an area you want to be. That's partially telling of areas (like my own neighborhood) that just don't pencil out in the positive. As well, common sense dictates with real estate: touch it, walk it, say "Hello" to the neighbors, etc.

On the other hand, with video calls, 3D software, drones, and analytics,

I'm not so sure common sense applies here. If you can divorce yourself from the worry by hiring a property manager, it's really just numbers. You don't need that emotional connection spoon fed from real estate agents. That can be detrimental when evaluating income property.

If the goal is to have passive income, a rental property can give you just that, *plus* the future possibility of appreciation somewhere down the line. But with the 1% rule, you don't have to worry or think about appreciation.

The next factor in favor of rental properties is expenses.

When you buy a rental property, everything you spend fixing the place, maintaining it, and managing it, are deductions. If it's your primary residence, you can't write-off any of those expenses.

An income property is just a business. Like any business, everything you spend that is considered "ordinary, necessary, and reasonable" (the IRS' criteria) to conduct that business is a write-off. As a landlord you spend money marketing, leasing, cleaning, and repairing. These are all direct deductions from your rental income.

People love to say they're sick of renting and throwing their money down the toilet. With a mortgage, they claim they can write it off and build equity.

This is only partially true.

When you live in the home you own, you can only write off the interest portion of your personal residence's mortgage, not the principal payment; and only up to the first $750,000 in mortgage debt.

You can, however, write off your property taxes. That is indeed a huge benefit. But it's also a huge cost. In Los Angeles our property taxes are 1.25%. A $750,000 home has a $9,375 bill every single year. Slide over to Texas. Property taxes are over double that, at 2.7%. Apparently everything *is* bigger in Texas.

When you own your primary residence, any maintenance is not a write-off. You eat all of those expenses just keeping the lawn green, garage clean, and the house from falling over.

If you do major *improvements* (not maintain, but upgrade), such as add a newer kitchen, redo a bathroom or knock out a wall; you've changed the actual value of the house.

You can't write off upgrades either. But because they are classified as improvements, they add to the cost basis of your house. This comes into play when you eventually sell. But not until, and if, you sell. It's potentially risky; a lot of people end up losing their flannel shirts trying to increase home values with improvements on their residences.

As long as you live in, and own the house, upgrades are expenses you pay the debt on (if financing those renovations) or simply have to eat until, and if, you sell.

What if there's no profit? A loss is a loss. There's no financial benefit to a $95,000 new open-concept, floor-to-ceiling glass kitchen if you can't recoup the cost of that at some time in the future. And sounds like you'll need a lot of Windex.

When you rent your residence, you get to pass all the responsibility to your landlord. Leaks, creaks, cracks, breakdowns, whatever - all are included in your rent. Make a single call and it gets fixed. As property taxes rise you don't have to worry. If there's an HOA assessment or you're in a gated community, you don't have to concern yourself with fees and charges. You can get on with your life, not worrying if the roof caves in or there's a water-heater leak.

The final reason it makes more sense to rent than buy is depreciation.

Depreciation is a large write-off multiplier because it's not a real expense you have to spend any money on.

Pay attention to this. It's one of the best reasons to own income property, effectively giving you free income.

When you own residential income property you get to take a large phantom deduction. You get the benefit of it, as if you spent it, but no money is actually leaving your wallet. This is calculated by dividing the property's value by 27.5. That result is the amount you can deduct every year you own the property.

A duplex that you purchased for $800,000 as income property has a yearly deduction of $29,090.

$800,000 purchase / 27.5 (depreciation figure) = $29,090

You don't actually spend this $29,090. But you get to record this expense just as if it were money you spent.

Another way to look at it is that the first $29,090 you make in rent on this $800,000 duplex, you can just put in your pocket tax-free. There's no profit in the eyes of the IRS. It's completely wiped out by depreciation. You can't depreciate your principal residence at all. Zip.

The theory is that, according to the IRS, the real property (so the building and everything except the dirt it sits on) has a useful life of 27.5 years if it's for residential purposes. If it's commercial, like retail stores, then this number is 39.

I think any real estate investor would strongly agree that there isn't a real "depreciation" in the asset. The value of the rental house or the duplex isn't declining in utility value by 1/27th of its purchase price every year. That's absurd. Sure, the market value may fluctuate, but a house has economic value that remains somewhat constant or even increases.

This is why this allowable deduction is so incredibly valuable to real estate investors. It's also why, for me personally, I bring in large amounts of rental real estate income, yet record only tiny fractions of it for tax purposes.

Here's a small case in point:

I have a side rental property business with a business partner from college. We are now on our 3rd cash flowing income property. Although we have always been cash flow positive (which provides monthly distributions to both of us), the depreciation on these houses (Nashville, Joshua Tree, Palm Springs) has always brought every single house into the negative.

We have effectively avoided taxes all together by legally following the IRS' guidelines. The government makes you take this depreciation. You can't avoid it.

Here are the numbers:

We paid $265,000 for a Nashville townhome.

$265,000 purchase / 27.5 = $9,636 yearly depreciation

Our gross revenue in rents per year was $23,304 for college students attending Vanderbilt University. Once we subtracted HOA dues, property taxes, maintenance, repairs, AND distributions to ourselves as partners, we came close to $9,000 in profit.

$9,000 profit - $9,636 depreciation = $636 loss

That $9,636 depreciation figure wiped out any real income. Gone. In fact, we show a loss. That loss gets carried to our personal tax returns where we get to claim it as a deduction.

We paid $220,000 for a Joshua Tree house.

$220,000 purchase / 27.5 = $8,000 yearly depreciation

Revenue was about $25,000 a year. After mortgage, property taxes, expenses as an Airbnb, and again, distributions to us as partners, we ended up with roughly $5,000 a year.

$5,000 profit - $8,000 depreciation = $3,000 loss

Again, no paper income.

Here's where it makes sense to own more than one property. We paid $463,000 for a Palm Springs house.

$463,000 purchase price / 27.5 = $16,836 yearly depreciation

Revenue is over $75,000 a year for this one due to its seasonal vacation appeal. But with large short-term rental expenses, taxes, *and distributions to ourselves (profit)*, we show a loss. We can't avoid it.

We get to deduct $16,836 on this property alone, as well as carry over the losses from Joshua Tree and Nashville. Negative.

The LLC that we formed to own these properties has a bottom line that is a negative figure. No to taxes. Yes to cash. Time to run for office.

I reiterate, this is *with* monthly partnership distributions to us. Those distributions are tax-free due in large part to depreciation. We are making money. We have profit. But due largely to this 27.5 rule, we don't show any.

If you are buying a house for your family and you love it and it's not an investment per se; if you can afford to buy it and not be stressed about the monthly payments, upkeep and emergencies; then buy that house if the narrative of buying that house is important to you. I get it.

But if it's automatic, monthly wealth you're after, take that same purchasing power for your own residence, that same amount of cash and debt and leverage it with income properties. That's my advice.

Collect stealth wealth, automatically. Lend those income houses to families who need to rent them. Let property managers solve the toilets and trash and send you monthly checks. And then go rent whatever house you want to live anywhere you want.

Untether.

There's a great story to be told from what else you can create, make, explore, and discover when you have financial freedom and permission to live your best life.

9

Trust Delaware For Wealth

"Self-Trust is the first secret of success."

- Ralph Waldo Emerson

My mom owned income property in San Bernardino county (CA) for over two decades. She was growing frustrated and stressed with her high-maintenance tenants. She wasn't using a management company. She was retired (still is). Increasingly, she fielded calls from her renters with demands for repairs.

Turns out her tenants were taking advantage of her. They were breaking things, misusing appliances, causing water damage, etc., and she was picking up the bill every time. I don't think this situation was intentional. But neither my mom nor the tenants understood the proper relationship or responsibility between landlady and renter.

The modest house that was supposed to bring passive income in her golden years was turning out to be a burden: sourcing contractors, calling the insurance company, and more importantly, spending money on expenses that were not legitimately hers.

She should have just hired a property management company to take care of everything. Although there's a price for that (anywhere between 8-12%). But she may have saved that in rent increases and on expenses she wasn't responsible for. Not to mention the headache.

I didn't want an additional job, but she's my mom. I agreed to take over the management of the house, deal directly with the tenants, and deposit rent checks into her bank account.

After clarifying who pays for which repairs and maintenance, and finally increasing the rent, we had a system that worked smoothly for about 4 years. I automated it as much as I could. But when you're a landlord without a management company in place, everything is fine until it isn't.

I said "No" to a lot of things, from garbage disposal to toilet clog to malfunctioning dishwasher, respectfully defining for them the difference between urgent and important. And I raised the rent every year a modest 2-3% in line with inflation.

This allowed my mom to say "Yes" to more important things in her life.

My mom was eventually getting $1,850 a month rent checks. She owned the home and had paid off the mortgage. But she still had property taxes at $5,000 a year, liability and homeowners insurance at $1,000, and roughly $250 a year in miscellaneous repairs - all write-offs to reduce her taxable income, but expenses nonetheless.

She was netting about $1,300 a month. Not bad considering her depreciation expense allowed her to keep most of that; there's that magic 27.5 number again.

Now, you know I love income real estate. I spent the last chapter singing the anthem to the 1% rule, Roofstock, and the benefits of income property. But for some people, including my mom, there comes a time when you want to off-load properties.

My mom simply wants lifetime monthly income she can depend on without the crowded mental space of actual tenants. She wants to know she won't outlive her money. This is a common concern among members of the older generation - which is the fastest growing demographic in the world.

You may not be of that age. But you can still benefit from knowing what I'm about to share with you. Because whether you're about to buy your 1st income property or 30th, there will come a time when you don't want to have it anymore, for whatever reason, financial or other.

The big downside to selling income property is taxes. All of those incredible benefits I mentioned in the last chapter now come home to roost. Those profitable expenses you depreciated over the years now have to get added *back* when you go to sell. They are *recaptured*. Depending on your tax bracket this is a massive taxable event.

This is why one rule of income properties is to never sell. Ever.

Sometimes when I look back at all of the real estate I've purchased over the years, I wish I had simply never sold. Chaos theory allows for infinite options, so I don't dwell on the choose-your-own-adventure paths not taken. But it's interesting to think what would have happened had the real estate butterfly flapped its wings in a different direction.

A popular strategy among real estate investors is to incorporate the voiced reaction to cold: BRRR, or **B**uy, **R**enovate, **R**ent, and **R**efinance. In other words, buy an undervalued income property, fix it up to attract good tenants, collect rent, establish it as a solid income business, and then refinance it (rather than sell).

With the new refinance you can pull out equity and go activate something else with the money. You avoid the capital gains and depreciation recapture entirely. But you still have the property.

You've likely heard of a 1031-Exchange. Most people know it colloquially as "rolling over" the profits from one house to another. That's it in a nutshell.

With a 1031-Exchange you sell one income property and replace it with another income property. So there's no real "sale." And if there's no sale, there's no taxes. You simply swapped properties. But there are time limits on how quickly this must be done; you must identify the replacement property within 45 days of the date of sale.

What happens if you can't move that fast or the market isn't on your side? Often people have no choice but to take the cash and pay huge tax on realized profit.

There's a strategy that even real estate industry pros aren't aware of. And it fits in very nicely with the banking mindset. I'm excited to share this with you as I couldn't believe it worked until I stumbled upon it myself.

It's called a Delaware Statutory Trust (DST). Tuck that away while I finish the story about my mom.

I put my mom's house on the market and sold it. As a reminder, she was collecting $1,850 gross monthly rent, and after expenses would end up with about $1,300 in income. These figures are important, as you'll see. Math can make you wealthy.

I signed her up for a 1031-Exchange (I recommend Old Republic Exchange in North Carolina). The house sold and all funds went to the exchange. Then, during that 45-day identification period for a replacement property, I simply signed her up for a DST on the platform, RealtyMogul.

Within a month she already received her first $2,200 check as her income from the DST. This wasn't gross revenue. This was her income after all expenses. It was hers to keep.

Furthermore, she avoided all capital gains taxes and recapture she would have had from selling her house, saving her over $80,000. Now those 80,000 employees of hers get promoted to a new spacious office rather than stand in the unemployment line.

She is now receiving $900 more a month in actual net cash than she was with her physical house. It's 100% passive, 100% automatic, and 100% Excedrin free.

Plus, she starts a new depreciation tax schedule which essentially knocks out a large portion of that $2,200 cash in the eyes of Uncle Sam. That's because a DST is a very special vehicle.

My mom is literally a fractional owner of the deed on a large portfolio of commercial properties. And since she is legally an "owner" she gets the same benefits anyone would with their own income property, but proportionate to her fraction.

The DST is managed entirely by institutional level professionals. There's nothing she could do even if she wanted to. Hands off.

Once the DST time period has ended in about 10 years, she will get all of that original money back - the money from her San Bernardino house sale - plus whatever appreciation she's gained in the DST over the decade.

But now, since the DST is selling, she'll have to finally pay all of those deferred taxes and depreciation recapture. The piper once again returns. He always seems to find his way back. Probably all those rat droppings.

Here's the strategy: Keep the piper on a wild goose chase forever. Never sell.

My mom can exchange out of this DST and into a new DST. And so on, and on, and on, enjoying the increasing income and avoiding the taxes. She just keeps exchanging and never has to worry about anything more than pulling out her phone to snapshot her monthly mobile deposits. This leaves more time for her to leave confusing and embarrassing comments on my Facebook posts.

Essentially, hundreds of people like my mom are selling within the same window of time but either can't find a replacement property in their 1031 exchange or simply don't want to own one on their own. The DST is considered a legally acceptable replacement property.

My mom's specific DST is a large group of over 50 commercial buildings with stalwart tenants like Walgreens, CVS, Tractor Supply, Dollar General, and Hobby Lobby. That's a common portfolio mix for a DST.

If you remember chapter 6 on dividend stocks, you see why a DST might include these types of companies. DSTs focus on income, not appreciation. They too live the *Make Bank* lifestyle.

I discovered this out of panic. Earlier, I sold an Austin loft I had bought after a couple of years attending/speaking at the SXSW Film Festival in Texas with my movies. I managed it myself, had great tenants, and great profits. No complaints for the most part.

But I wanted to sell so I could buy something near me in L.A. I was looking at 4-plexes in the quickly gentrifying West Adams area near Culver City. To avoid those capital gains taxes and depreciation recapture I had been enjoying, I entered into a 1031-Exchange.

The Austin loft's sales proceeds went to the Exchange, not me, so I wouldn't be taxed. There was no "sale." That 45-day countdown began and I immediately hunted for a replacement. I searched, looked, made numerous offers, and was even in escrow twice. But nothing. Everything fell out. And time didn't slow down.

Day 41. Day 42. Day 43...

I was calculating that I would owe about $100,000 in taxes. That's a lot of equity to lose in a property I've patiently let bake with Texas BBQ sauce all those years without burning.

But with professor Google to the rescue, I stumbled upon DSTs. So I jumped into two separate ones, one in North Austin and one in Pensacola, Florida. I split my Austin loft's sales value right down the middle, 50% to each DST.

50% was allocated to 422 apartments in North Austin.

And 50% went to 224 apartments in Pensacola, FL.

With DSTs and 1031-Exchanges, you're allowed to exchange from one property to many, or many to one. It doesn't matter. As long as you're swapping out the total value for value, you completely avoid taxes.

Within a month, I was immediately pulling in more monthly income than I did when I thought I was a brilliant real estate tycoon with the Austin loft. And now I didn't have to replace the leaking water heater, or the A/C unit that cost me $6,500 to have craned on top of a 9-story building.

I still own the North Austin DST that came from 50% of the Austin loft sale. With precision it just airdrops cash into my account every month as my share of the income from the DST portfolio.

The Pensacola, Florida DST that came from the other 50% of the loft sale was sold 2 years later. The managers of that DST saw an opportunity to sell it for a nice profit much sooner than anticipated. It wasn't supposed to sell for another 5 years. But profit came knocking and I wasn't manning the door.

I immediately had to make a decision for my portion of the profits - a good problem.

Option 1: I could simply take the funds, pay capital gains tax and depreciation recapture. Now I would have access, once again, to cash. My employees could come home to the L.A. factory ready to be placed elsewhere. But I would lose too many of them in the process.

Option 2: I could exchange into a physical income property that I would own 100%. Using Roofstock, for example, I could just buy up as many properties that met the 1% rule and continue leveraging my rental portfolio. This was a viable option for me.

Option 3: My third choice was to simply exchange into yet *another* DST.

Once again, I searched and looked. Because I still intuitively like the idea of having my own rental house that I can drive by and see. But you've seen this movie before and know how it ends.

Day 42. Day 43. Day 44. DST.

To avoid the large amount of taxes, which by now is the sum of the original Austin loft plus the gains in the sale of the Pensacola DST, I chose option #3: I entered another DST.

This time the DST was a large portfolio of commercial property, which I currently own, fractionally. And once again, I'm earning more passive income that comes with depreciation to substantially reduce the taxes.

I was only netting about $600 a month from the original Austin loft after Texas' Texas-sized property taxes (2.7%), maintenance, repairs, HOA, and mortgage. So it was much smaller than the $1,900 a month I was collecting in rent.

But with the DSTs that I shifted this exact equity into from the 1031-Exchange, I was immediately receiving $1,100 a month take-home, after all expenses. That number has now grown to a little over $1,300 a month, which I still receive to this day without missing a beat.

In the end, with math and maneuvering I've doubled my take-home cash ($600 a month converted into $1,300 a month), and it's as passive as it gets. Tax free too!

I joined every one of these DSTs through RealtyMogul. They can equally be done on other platforms, 1031Crowdfunding probably being the most well-known. I just haven't consummated a relationship with anyone else, although I did briefly have a few dates with others. It's not them. It's me.

I love RealtyMogul's team of founders, executives, and how circumspect they are with their deals. They also have a tight relationship with ExchangeRight, which in my book is the best DST portfolio manager in the business - strong track record, conservative, and a focus on wealth preservation with regular monthly income. They're bankers.

The two downsides to DSTs are liquidity and appreciation. This shouldn't affect your banker's mindset, however, as you are designing your financial life to be automatic and passive. DSTs are the pure definition of this. Second, you can't sell or transfer out until management finds an exit they agree makes sense for their investors.

So what if you aren't in a 1031-Exchange and want the benefit of a DST? And what if you want something like a DST but you additionally want the benefit of *accelerated appreciation*?

Is that even possible? Cake *and* eating? Sounds too good to be true.

The next chapter will introduce you to a place for exactly that. It's where I currently place most of my real estate dollars, continuing to encourage those loyal and hardworking employees to become better bankers.

10

Multiply Money With Multi-families

*"Repeat after me: real estate provides the highest returns,
the greatest values and the least risk."*
- Armstrong Williams

If you've ever lived in a large apartment complex of roughly 100 units or more you've paid your rent to someone like me.

These sprawling multifamily buildings are generally garden style with nice lawns and walkways. They might have some pools or tennis courts. There's typically a lobby or office for leasing and events. There's often an exercise room, outdoor play area for kids, and runs for dogs. Parking is communal, outside or underground. And they're geographically desirable to commerce, business parks, freeways, and schools. Idyllic.

When I produced *Duck Dynasty*, this was the exact type of complex I lived in as part of our crew and staff housing for the TV show. You didn't have to calculate much to realize the owners had turned the place into an automatic money machine. With units stacked on top of each other 3 floors high there was a total of 338 units spread out over 20 acres.

When you factor in the $1,200 a month each unit took in per month on average, that's over $400,000 a month in revenue. The place was booked solid. Some of our crew members even had to bunk together.

My research tells me the owners purchased and built this all for roughly $3.2 million back in 2008. That's what is currently on the tax rolls. If I'm off, they got it for even less, since it's probably been reassessed.

As you learned from chapter 8 with the 1% rule for income properties, you'd only need $32,000 a month to make this a desirable deal based on that valuation. But it's pulling in over $400,000 a month at full occupancy. Economies of scale give this place its own stratospheric rule of 12.5x.

Even at a $16 million valuation (5x that $3.2M investment), this would still make a huge return. That's probably why it's not for sale. I inquired. Twice. Because even at 90% occupancy, that pulls in $365,000 a month.

And believe me when I tell you that real estate in West Monroe isn't selling like hotcakes. Real estate is relatively inexpensive there, selling more like slow-cooked beans. Some of our cast members had homes that would have been $10 million estates in L.A. They built them for 1/20th of that.

Multifamily living communities are highly profitable for the owners. The community is almost never owned by one individual. They are most commonly formed and owned by a *syndicate* of people all pooling their money to buy such family housing.

These are very different from the bridge loans for builder projects where you invest in the debt and hold the mortgage (chapter 7). Those investments are solely to collect the interest on mortgages. You are limited to making exactly what the interest rate is and no more.

With multifamily deals you acquire a mortgage *and* put up the cash down payment, no different from buying a single house on Roofstock or Redfin. Same thing, but multiply the numbers by 1,000, or even 10,000.

You receive numerous benefits owning income-producing real estate rather than just investing in it. But with that comes increased risk. With more risk comes more reward.

First, as a fractional, equity owner, you not only collect your passive, monthly checks, you also collect a potentially substantial one when you sell 3, 5, or 7 years later. That's the goal, to have an appreciation sale in the not too distant future.

This is one way multifamily syndicates are different from DSTs. They not only set up regular income, they position themselves for multiplying your investment at the end of the term.

As the owner you share in this eventual sale, which is already in motion the day you buy. The exit strategy is indicative of all syndicates, which is to get in-and-out within specific time frames. Owners plan for this on the day they join the syndicate.

Second, as an equity owner, you are entitled to all of the tax benefits. You take that profitable depreciation deduction with the generous 27.5 calculation. This effectively boosts your real returns since most of it is saved from being taxed.

The rates you earn on these deals vary depending on how quick the turnaround time is; how undervalued a property is at acquisition; and how solid the business plan is to stabilize the property with attractive, fully occupied rents. And factor in a successful exit.

A lot has to happen. But it's not wizardry. It's a formulaic rinse-and-repeat process that real estate entrepreneurs have been taking advantage of for as long as there has been real estate. Even New York's Empire State building was purchased back in the 60s with a syndicate in $10,000 chunks for each owner/investor.

As a rule, I rarely buy these deals unless I'm averaging 20% a year over the hold period.

Here are the three important factors to observe:

- Internal Rate of Return (IRR)
- Equity Multiple
- Cash-on-Cash.

And here's a recent deal I purchased in Texas to demonstrate these factors:

- IRR = 20.6%.
- Equity Multiple = 1.8x
- Cash-on-Cash = 11.4%

Let's start with the 11.4% cash-on-cash. This is the income component of these deals. It's automatic and passive. It represents the checks or deposits you receive every month as a return on your ownership. This is simply the aggregate of rent rolls from all units minus the expenses, including management and operating costs.

I invested $25,000 in this deal. So over the 3-year hold period before the sale, it is forecast that I will receive an average of $2,850 a year in deposits, each of those 3 years (11.4% of $25,000 = $2,850). That's the cash return on my cash investment.

In theory, if the property never sells that's the only number you care about. It's the consistent cash you want in the first place. This would be similar to a DST in that respect.

The equity multiple is forecast at 1.8x. Its name is accurate as it's just a multiple of your equity. For this deal, that's $25,000 x 1.8 = $45,000. When the 3 year period is up, if the property sells for its projections, I will have walked away from this sale with a total of $45,000 in my account. This is the final, total sum of all money - my initial $25,000, all the cash I received every month until sale, and then my portion of the appreciation upon sale. The equity multiple ties it all into a nice total calculation.

The Internal Rate of Return (IRR) is technically confusing but in general is similar to annual percentage rate (APR). The reason it's different is that it factors in the time it takes you to physically receive your money in the future, but discounted in present day value. This is because with these deals, you are without your initial investment from day one. But the way the money comes back changes over the course of the deal from increased monthly payments to the final sale. These different amounts coming at different times make it difficult to state a true APR, as with a savings account.

If you invest $25,000 on January 1 and get back your $25,000 plus another $25,000 on December 31, you'd have a 100% IRR. It's simple here because it's a one year time period and you double your money, which is 100%. So it's equivalent to the annual percentage rate in this case.

But if this were a 5-year return-period and you received the same $25,000 profit on top of your $25,000 return, this would roughly be a 20% IRR. The

IRR is much lower than 100%, yet the return is identical. IRR accounts for the length of time. I'm simplifying here because I'm removing the variables of the monthly cash-on-cash.

This is why all 3 of these go hand in hand, each revealing different parts of the deal. Combined, they're sort of a Justice League of super numbers that remind you that time is money. And even if a deal looks incredible because you'll triple your money, if that takes 15 years, that's not a fantastic deal in my book. The IRR will reveal this, as it will be low.

Here's my own little question-hack to myself: Can I double my money in 5 years or less? That's just another way of saying, can I make 20% a year.

If the answer is "Yes," I'm in. The Texas example above doesn't technically double my money; it's a 1.8 multiple, not a 2x. But it happens within only 3 years, which *more than doubles* my money during a similar 5 year period. A 1.8 multiple divided by 3 years equates to a .6 multiple each year. And a .6 multiple x 5 years = 3x. This deal is equivalent to tripling my money in 5 years. That, I'll take.

The general rule in the stock market is that you double your money every 7 years over the long run. That's with simple index investing, using a buy and hold strategy. That is equivalent to a .28x of your money every year. This Texas deal above is a .6x every year, which is more than double the stock market. Both stocks and real estate have risks, so I prefer taking risk for higher reward.

To find a syndicate there are two main options depending on if you're accredited or not. Fortunately, syndicates are plentiful. You'll find dozens of them accessible in your own area.

If you're a non-accredited investor, you want to go to places like MeetUp, BiggerPockets, EventBrite, or FaceBook and find real estate investing groups. These scheduled gatherings are open to anyone who is interested in learning about real estate. And usually there are several syndicates that are currently funding. They usually just go by the name of "multifamily investing" or "apartment investing."

Many of the real estate investors at these functions are still learning and have day jobs. But they attend to network and hear from scheduled speakers.

The SEC says that non-accredited investors can't be advertised to, and that you have to have a *prior relationship* with the syndicate. This is why these are all done via these meet-up groups. Once you join and mingle, you're allowed to ask about syndicates since you're no longer a stranger.

You never have to join a syndicate if you don't want to. There's absolutely no pressure or sales pitches. The good syndication deals actually discourage people because they only have so much room in the limited partnerships or LLCs set-up to take in new owners/investors. Good deals always fill up. There's no issue finding money.

This is a key principle in commercial real estate: Finding money is easy. It's finding an attractive deal that is difficult. If you can't find the money, there's something wrong with the numbers. Plain and simple.

This is the reason you can make insane amounts of money traveling around the country to source and find these deals. It's very lucrative. But that's a lot of leg-work. It's why people like me living the *Make Bank* lifestyle simply want a nice deck to digest while on the elliptical, financials to scan over black coffee, and a webinar to watch while sunning shirtless on the patio. That's all I need to make a decision to shift my money into cruise control.

You absolutely must evaluate these deals and understand exactly how they work. It's uncomplicated, but like anything, will be foreign to the uninitiated. Once you've done your due diligence, there's nothing to do even if you wanted to, other than get quarterly reports of the rent rolls.

Now, if you are an accredited investor, the SEC allows you to be advertised to publicly (the Internet). Regulation D 506(c) is what has spawned crowdsourcing of syndicates at sites like RealtyMogul (my favorite, and where I bought into my DSTs in chapter 9) and CrowdStreet (my 2nd favorite where I have half-a-dozen multifamily apartments and senior housing deals).

There are dozens of syndicate platforms online. As with everything else on the Internet, the access and ease to evaluate the options is convenient and efficient. You never need to leave your computer to invest and become an owner.

Even if you're not accredited, I recommend going to CrowdStreet and RealtyMogul and signing up. Click through their deal flow, watch the webinars and read the decks. You will quickly learn what deals look like. These platforms are all investors themselves so they don't allow just any syndicate to promote. They're selective.

I find RealtyMogul to be more cautious, with very few projects available every quarter, if that. But when they come up, they're almost always winners, in my book. They scan hundreds of deals every quarter and select less than 1% to avail themselves to investors. Over the last 7 years they've completed deals on over 16,000 apartment units.

Crowdstreet is also circumspect, but allows more deals on their platform with slightly looser standards. Sometimes I can't keep up with their volume.

This all starts with a real estate entrepreneur who has boots on the ground to source properties. She is called a Sponsor. She walks the tracks looking for undervalued properties in submarkets with growing populations, increasing demand, and maybe a shortage of decent housing.

She ideally looks at the size of a project for its economies of scale; the unit mix for potentially lower vacancies, physical condition for inexpensive upgrades, mismanagement to explain lack of tenant retention, tired landscaping, and other obvious missteps.

The most important factor for her is to add simple, obvious value with as little money as possible. Syndicates appropriately call this "value add."

Rather than a deal where the buildings are falling over, or equally, where the place is Class-A and pristine beautiful, the sponsor wants something in between, some meat on the bone (but not too much or too little). Since she's already planning for the eventual sale, she wants to get an undervalued property that masks its real potential. It's a diamond in the rough.

A deal with attractive style and economic level is a Class-B property. It's not the most expensive or high-end (Class-A). The economy can wipe out those renters. And it's not the most dilapidated (Class-C), which can attract sub-par renters. It's in the middle of the road - affordable but not too affordable. Nice, but not too nice. Sort of Goldilocks.

Maybe the current owner of the apartment complex has neglected some maintenance. The complex may have aging appliances or periodic leaks. It's common to see fatigued management who isn't effective in building community pride or sprucing up vacated units to raise rents. Maybe their turnover is slow. Maybe they're losing months instead of a week for carpeting, painting, keying, and leasing.

The property may also just be dated. The style and decor might be yesterday's unfavorable design. This keeps the current tenants, but when the lease is up, newer places across the street look better and more desirable. They don't have the sign and logo carved out of wood from the '70s sitting at the entrance. These relative small vanities make a difference in rental rates. People will call this place home.

A smart sponsor wants to come in, paint the units, add new dishwashers, and throw in new baseboards. Then maybe add a fun communal area outside with a new grilling station and a jungle gym for kids. And what about landscaping? What about re-paving the crumbling parking lot? What about new lamp posts for the walkways?

It doesn't have to be outrageous. It's often simple upgrades that help keep up morale and increase occupancy.

Ultimately, the only revenue such a project generates is rents. Therefore the goal is to simultaneously increase occupancy and increase rents. Making the place nicer is the easiest way to accomplish that.

When you think about it, we all just live in boxes made out of nails and boards (and go out that way too). But we assign value, and pay for that value, based on the arrangement and quality of those nails and boards. Some people become lazy or focus on other things in life. Nothing wrong with that. But for making money, it's pretty straightforward to update the cosmetics.

Swapping managers is also common. A new management company typically breathes fresh life into the culture and ecosystem. They invigorate the neighborhood and engender spirit with pool parties, tenant referral bonuses, and free months' rent for new tenants. Just having food trucks come around once a month is something that costs nothing other than planning. Neighbors finally meet each other. They continue to enjoy where they live. They tell others.

Here's a hypothetical scenario.

Suppose a sponsor is evaluating a 20-year old multifamily property for potential offer. Its occupancy has declined to 85% due to disintegration. The sponsor knows that boosting the occupancy just 5 percent to 90% will drastically change profits. On a typical 300-unit complex at say $1,200 a month lease rates, increasing occupancy just 5% is filling 15 more units. Doesn't sound like much on a 300 unit property. But those 15 units at the same $1,200 lease rates is another $216,000 per year.

Now imagine those 15 units were improved at a cost of $7,000 per door (painting, new cabinet handles, new floor, and indoor laundry). Now they can command higher rents of say $1,600 a month for these higher-end units with their own washers and dryers.

The goal would be to continue to upgrade units as leases expire and boost all those doors in say 3 years' time to $1,500 a month. If they achieve a 95% occupancy, they're now at $5.13 million per year (285 units x $1,500 x 12). And in this example the current owners are operating at $3.67 million per year (255 units x $1,200 x 12).

Of course, that $7,000 per door/unit has to be absorbed. That is $2.1 million to eventually turn all 300 units. But this amounts to the total Value-Add. This $2.1 million is part of the financials and added on top of the purchase price in factoring the deal. The sponsor knows this $2.1 million is well spent if she sees several exit strategies well above this $2.1 million plus purchase price plus desired appreciation.

And in actuality, the sponsor will get this hypothetical property for more than $2.1 Million *below* market value anyway. In real estate, they say you make your money when you buy.

The larger a project the more attractive it is. Adding new bathroom sinks or ceiling fans for that many units will be more economical when purchased in volume. Ditto for contractors, etc. Deals can be made directly with manufacturers when you're buying 100 dishwashers. Your fixed costs go down. You amortize over more doors. A $20,000 pool resurfacing job across 300 doors = $67 per unit. Doesn't sound so expensive in order to give everyone a shimmering new pool.

Almost all the deals I have been involved in tend to get occupancy to the 94-98% levels before exit. Most of those are a 5% climb in tenants, all done with simple value-ads.

Once all of these boxes tick off for the sponsor, she now has to underwrite the deal. She has to run the numbers, contact banks for mortgage financing, meet with contractors, management companies, appraisers, etc.

If she's confident the numbers make sense, she makes an off-market offer to the owners of the property. This is how she buys built-in profit by not competing on the open market with other buyers.

Once there's an accepted offer, escrow begins. Escrow is when the sponsor now takes the terms she's negotiated and goes to get funding. That's where you, the owner/investor, comes in.

You attend a local real estate meet-up or Zoom meeting where she speaks on multifamily investing in general. If you like what she is saying, she'll have decks and webinar links for you to check out her latest deal. These materials outline her entire research and financial projections.

You also want to make sure the sponsor has some skin in the game. If they don't have at least 5% of the equity bucket, I'm rarely interested. They'll tell you it's because they have other projects and are diversifying across all of their deals. This may be true. But for me, I want to know they are personally invested with more than just their big toe. So if a deal is for $100 million and the equity portion is $20 million ($80 million in debt with a mortgage), then I want to know the Sponsor (or the Sponsor's company in most cases) is in for

$1 million (5% of $20M). Now I see both her feet, which she'll need with the work ahead.

The exits and sales are somewhat built in. Savvy sponsors know when to start speaking with institutional investors (pensions, municipalities, family offices, funds), banks, brokers, and other real estate syndicates. Once the project achieves a certain level of success and stabilization on the books, it will be attractive for others looking for good cash flow. That's what it mostly boils down to. When the numbers can be achieved, the syndicate will have numerous choices.

A lot of large funds and REITS (Real Estate Investment Trusts) want good performing projects. They don't want to develop. That's not their business model. They want high-quality places that will generate immediate and dependable cash flow over the next 15 to 20 years. Fortunately, the syndicate just did all the hard work to get it to that performance level, as I imagine was done with our *Duck Dynasty* housing. You as an investor get to benefit for helping to fund the hunting and gathering. The institutional funds just want to sit down and enjoy the feast.

Speaking of *Duck Dynasty*, one of the TV show's editors, Chris Collins, is one of these sponsors. Chris now has a real estate investing company, Amity Cash Flow (AmityCashFlow.com). He and his partners scout locations all over the U.S. forming and funding syndicates. They perform all the same steps I just outlined above (and then some), and welcome non-accredited investors on many of their deals. I highly recommend reaching out to Chris if you need a place to start or can't find a suitable meetup group. I'm currently invested in one of his deals, a 268-unit value-add apartment complex in San Antonio, TX.

Multifamily investing is not rocket science, unless rocket science involves painting rockets and selling them for double in 5 years. Then it's a lot like rocket science. You're probably even invested in some of these via your 401K, IRA, or ETF.

There are syndicates for every type of real estate - commercial office space, medical buildings, senior housing, new hotels, shopping centers, industrial, public storage, etc. You don't have to deal solely in multifamily buildings.

But from my experience and research, buying into Class-B value-add multifamily apartments appear to be the lowest risk of all. I was reminded of that right after the height of the COVID-19 pandemic. Office buildings were decimated. Hotels went completely dark. But everyone still needed to rent. And with Class-B, you're stuck in the middle such that even if you lose tenants who downsize to Class-C, you equally gain the Class-A renters who need to downsize to Class-B. Being stuck in the middle isn't so bad.

I do, however, own two senior-housing syndicates, one in Portland, Oregon, and one in Hadley, Massachusetts. With the growing older demographic, I think senior-housing will be a fast growing space in syndication. And to me, these are essentially multifamily housing, but for civilized tenants who don't jump off balconies into the pool, punch holes through walls after losing a game of beer pong, or break stair banisters from making TikTok videos.

I also own one storage facility syndicate. Unfortunately people just can't break their habit of buying more stuff than they need. And I can't break my habit of passively making piles of money.

11

Present Value Of Future Money

"Every time you borrow money, you're robbing your future self."

- Nathan W. Morris

A mortgage broker from the East coast flew out to Beverly Hills, CA to spend a couple weeks in our film production offices to learn the mechanics of movie financing.

I was partnered at the time with a gifted screenwriter and producer (our company made 7 movies).

The mortgage broker (let's call him Alex) never ended up investing in any of our films, but today we remain contacts. We share a love for finance, math, and movies. No hard feelings. 95% of investor meetings pan out this way.

Years later he called me asking for a favor. He was speaking with an unknown wannabe actor in L.A. (toss a small role anywhere; you'll hit several). He offered to pay me $1,000 just to take the actor out to lunch and give him some general advice.

This actor, who shall remain nameless, had just won the local lottery. But instead of selecting the $10 million upfront lump sum, he chose a schedule of payments over 30 years. After taxes and spread out over 360 months, it didn't feel like anything close to $10 million for him. He had other investment opportunities and wanted the benefit of several million immediately. But he was already on the payout schedule and couldn't reverse his decision.

Alex revealed to me that he had started a structured settlement company that bought these lottery contracts. He would get guaranteed monthly payouts from the state lottery commissions in exchange for making one-time payments to the winners.

This is done all the time when people win settlements from injuries as well. The insurance companies don't want to write one big multi-million dollar check. So they offer a "lifetime" of say $75,000 a year.

No one is going to complain about having $75,000 a year extra for the rest of their life. But think what you could do with say $1M right now. Depending on your strategy, you could turn that $1M into an automatic money machine of much more than $75,000 a year using any of the *Make Bank* strategies.

This is where my $1,000 lunch comes in. Since my friend was competing with numerous structured settlement companies for this actor's business, he wanted an edge. He told the actor that he had a friend in Hollywood.

So after calculating a robust profit for himself (and his investors), Alex makes an upfront offer so the actor gets paid a lump sum. It's a lot of money and a win-win for both parties' agendas.

The actor met me at my MTV offices in Santa Monica where I was producing a TV show. We walked a block, got lunch and talked about his chances of becoming a working actor (the typical steps, some obvious advice, and a few contacts with casting directors).

A week later I got my $1,000 check, and Alex has probably now made 1,000 times that, and is still collecting on this contract.

Alex is effectively a bank. He has brought the future value of someone's money into the present, without the help of H. G. Wells. And he takes his banker's fee for performing this time travel.

One of the last nails in the Craigslist lending coffin introduced me to this concept of structured settlements. A borrower (let's call her Raylien since that's her real name), contacted me wanting a $6,000 personal loan. She didn't have a job, had terrible credit history, and would have otherwise been a resounding "No." But she had collateral I found interesting: an insurance settlement.

According to her, she was at a gas station when she was 8. There was an accident, some kind of explosion, a fire, and some kind of medical complications - none obvious or visible to me.

Now 18, she showed me paperwork that awarded her $25,000 a year for 20 years. There were still 10 years left on the contract, so another $250,000 was still forthcoming.

She was currently working out a deal with one of these structured settlement companies for a $150,000 payout, just like my friend Alex did with the actor. Obviously, she had substantial collateral for a $6,000 loan. It seemed like a no-brainer.

But right on cue, as with most of my Craigslist clients, this one took the same course stage left: she stopped making payments and stopped returning my calls. *Gone Girl*.

Looking at her settlement agreement, I noticed that she was going to be getting her $150,000 from the settlement company any day now and I should just sit tight. She'd clearly have the money to pay me back soon.

But something whispered if this were the case, why would she ghost me? Was the settlement fake? Was I being scammed yet again?

After some light Googling I stumbled across UCC-1 Statements.
I quickly learned that by filing a Uniform Commercial Code Financing Statement, I "give notice," as a creditor, that I have a claim on personal property - in this case, the settlement contract.

It's scary to think in hindsight I never actually had any collateral. I was simply holding a copy of her settlement. But it's this UCC-1 statement that effectively puts a pseudo lien on the collateral, similar to real estate. The irony of her name being RayLIEN didn't escape me.

Not long thereafter, I received a call from a lawyer. He confirmed the details of the fiduciary relationship I had with Raylien. I answered all his questions, thinking that she was in a hospital or something similar, and that would explain why she was avoiding my attempts at communication.

Then the clouds parted and the sun shone. I heard these anxiety-reducing words: "We are cutting you a check for $9,500 (my $6,000 loan plus the loan shark rates I charged her)."

He went on to inform me that Raylien had an insurance settlement (as if I didn't know) and that all UCC-1 statements had to be paid off before she could receive any remaining funds.

The point of these two stories: The banker's economy benefits those who understand and monetize the difference between present and future values of money.

One of the most common and basic formulas in investment finance is NPV, or Net Present Value. It's one of the first formulas you learn in business school, and it's one I continue to use today in my mortgage business. It can be applied to almost anything for comparing the value of money today versus tomorrow.

Here it is in its most basic form:

$$NPV = FV / (1 + R)N$$

Spelled out, this means that the value of money today, right now (Net Present Value) is equal to the Future Value of the money divided by the sum of 1 plus the discount rate (interest rate of investment) to the exponential of time (number of years).

I know you're having algebra PTSD right now. I would too, if I weren't such a numbers dork. I'll make this more digestible.

To illustrate, if someone offered you $1M exactly 5 years from today or $500,000 today, which would you take?

Setting aside unknown sociological and psychological factors (such as not being able to control your spending), the NPV formula solves this problem without having to debate it. From a purely financial aspect it brings all of the numbers forward to the present so you can compare apples to apples (more fun than comparing Microsoft to Microsoft).

For instance, you know from chapters 5 and 6 you can earn a solid 8.6% compounded interest with stablecoins like USDC or GUSD at places like BlockFi or Celsius. The rate is fixed. So if you don't have access to that $1M for 5 years, you need to know what that $1M contract is worth today, to compare to the $500,000 cash today.

Half a million would be great right now. But is it a better or worse deal?

Plugging these numbers in the NPV formula, it looks like this:

NPV = $1,000,000 Future Value / (1 + .086 stablecoin rate)5 years

NPV = $1M / (1.086)5

NPV = $1M / 1.5106

NPV = $661,988

Today's value of that $1,000,000 in the future (using BlockFi's stablecoin investment of 8.6% as a barometer) = $661,988. All other factors being equal, those two amounts are identical. This equation gets complicated when you add tax rates and inflation so I simplify for the purpose of illustration.

The individual who guaranteed you $1M in 5 years doesn't have to set $1M aside today. She only has to set aside $661,988. It will turn into $1,000,000 on the day it is yours, if she's investing in stablecoins.

If she's using other methods throughout this book that give her 15% or 20%, etc., she can simply plug those numbers into the formula above. Same with the time period. What if this is 3 years? What if it is 7?

In investment terms, there is no difference between having $661,988 today or $1,000,000 in 5 years. If you have the cash today or the "contract" for it in 5 years, it has the precise same value.

Bankers love to make money off this formula because when one is skewed in either direction, there is money to be made. It's another form of spread or arbitrage for them.

If you were leaning toward the $500,000 now and couldn't wait 5 years, I would have stepped in as a 3rd party investor and sweetened the deal for you. I would have said, "I'll pay you $550,000 (giving you $50,000 more than originally offered) in exchange for buying that contract from you."

If you were close to accepting the original $500,000 you are now sold with the $50,000 kicker. I now have to wait 5 years for that $1,000,000 and I've lost the opportunity of investing my $550,000.

But I'm also happy because I just spent $550,000 to get $1,000,000 in the future for what I know from the NPV formula above costs $661,988 to get (again, sticking with stablecoins as the alternative at 8.6%). So I just made $111,988 by standing in lieu of a bank.

In Future Value terms, I made even more than $111,988 with this investment. Because if I were to take that $550,000, and, instead of giving it to you, bought stablecoins at BlockFi at 8.6%, I wouldn't come close to the $1M.

I can run the NPV formula in reverse to calculate this:

$$FV = NPV \times (1 + R)N$$

$$FV = \$550,000 \times (1.086)5$$

$$FV = \$550,000 \times 1.5106$$

$$FV = \$830,830.$$

If stablecoins are my only investing option, then you can see what a smart investment I made by buying your contract. Because investing $550,000 in stablecoins will bring me only $830,830 in 5 years time. But your contract just guaranteed me $1M. I will net a profit of almost $170,000 in Future Value in lieu of the $50,000 overage I had to spend for this opportunity.

Taking the nerd hat off, here's how this benefits you, the banker.

For various reasons, people need lump sum cash payments today. Whether you're Raylien with the insurance settlement, or the actor with the $10M lottery ticket, there are reasons one can't wait until tomorrow. They have some other form of value in the future that they want access to today.

And, as you learned above, this also works in reverse. Some people feel a lump sum now would cause them to spend it all, trigger major taxes, or negate some other agreement they have, as in a divorce. They'd rather have guaranteed payouts spread for 20 years.

CrowFly is one site (there are many) that sells these structured settlements. You can basically buy someone's insurance settlement by assuming ownership of their annuity from a major insurance company guaranteeing the payouts. Knowing how to calculate NPV, you can see which ones are profitable for you. Sticking with stablecoins, for example, it wouldn't make sense for you to buy a structured settlement on CrowFly if the calculation is less than 8.6%. But if you think rates of stablecoins will decline or you want to diversify, then you might consider those options.

There are many downsides to these, however, which is something to be aware of (and perhaps wary). You are locked in for the long haul, as most of these settlements are 10 years or more. And, depending on the discount rates, the economy could turn and you'd be better off in more liquid places like dividend stocks (chapter 6).

Plus you can't fractionally buy settlements at the moment, at least with ease. If you couldn't afford to take the entirety of someone's settlement, you'd have to form your own partnership of investors and have that partnership buy the annuity.

One way around this is with sites like YieldStreet or Cadence. I like both of these, but prefer YieldStreet. I've now been investing with Yieldstreet for over 5 years and have been pleased with their alternative and diversified options.

Cadence, however, has lower minimums of $500 per deal and is actively trying to remove the accredited investor requirement that these sites currently have.

At YieldStreet, I mostly invest in lawsuit settlements. These are "slip and fall," personal injury cases where I earn over 13%. YieldStreet works with companies such as LawCash which provides pre-settlement funding to plaintiffs during their court cases.

Sometimes plaintiffs can't wait 6 months to 2 years while their $200,000 injury case goes through the court system, if it even makes it to trial. LawCash knows, based on statistics, what the probability is of these cases settling. They know that a defendant might pay, for example, $110,000 to settle a $200,000 lawsuit and avoid trial.

Meanwhile, the plaintiff has medical bills to pay and wants to get on with life. The victim would be happy to take a guaranteed $50,000 right now in exchange for a much smaller percentage of any future award if it goes to trial. Plus, there's no guarantee the plaintiff will even win. LawCash takes that gamble.

YieldStreet will bundle these into 300 or 400 more similar cases and call it a fund. Now you have the benefit of diversification along with the upside that one of these cases may end up paying for all losers. The analysts/actuaries are skilled at factoring the odds, which gives you a sound interest rate for helping to fund these pre-settlements.

Here are the exact numbers I've had with YieldStreet on 8 deals I've completed:

I invested $10,000 in 493 pre-settlement advance cases as part of a $3.54M fund. YieldStreet estimated an IRR of roughly 13%. The fund returned 16.02% IRR to me and completed in 26 months.

Another one: I invested $5,000 in 163 cases as part of a smaller $1.4M fund. The IRR target was again 13%. Over 32 months, the fund completed and returned 15.92% IRR.

Then I bought 6 more just like the above, each at $5,000. Each returned more than the 13% projected payouts; most were also near 16%.

Even though I don't technically own the actual settlements, as I would with CrowFly, I can fractionally invest and still obtain a healthy, passive rate that has surpassed projections. And per my calculations, I'm making more with Yieldstreet than I would with CrowFly anyway, by almost double.

I also like these vehicles because they aren't correlated with the broader economy. Settlements, as an industry, have almost nothing to do with the stock market, real estate, or employment numbers. The payouts are also senior to any funds the plaintiffs may get should the case go to trial and have a large payout. You, the investor, gets paid first (just like the lawyers).

They say there's always a bull market somewhere. And this gives me another chance, in another sector, should outer space aliens invade our planet. And something tells me lawyers will figure out how to sue the little green guys when this happens.

Like it or not, our society is increasingly litigious and the courts are simply too busy to try every case. So settlements are the goal. And plaintiffs will gladly take the Net Present Value if you, the banker, are willing to take the Future Value.

This is an entire industry that most people have never heard of, that banks have known for years. I wish there was more access to this, but at the moment it's limited. Keep it on your radar. It will become more prevalent.

Other creative and alternative products along these lines are beginning to surface. Anytime there is I.P. (intellectual property) involved, there is a large discrepancy between present and future values.

You may have heard of the Bowie Bonds. In 1997 banker David Pullman securitized 25 of rock icon David Bowie's albums. He made all future royalties of those recordings available to investors who understand the future value of them. In exchange, David Bowie personally received $55 million.

On one level, present-future investing is the sole investing strategy of the entertainment and music industry; banking on 110 pages of typed paper or 45 minutes of audio to become the next billion dollar franchise.

You can even bank on Banksy. At Masterworks, you can invest a minimum of $1,000 in artwork from Andy Warhol, Keith Haring, Banksy, Claude Monet, Jean-Michel Basquiat, etc. You don't have to be accredited. You can divide your $1,000 into as little as $20 chunks and create your own blue chip fund of 50 different artists. It's a great approach to sharing in artwork appreciation.

Most people don't know that the art world has returned over *double* what the stock market (S&P 500 Index) has in the last 20 years. No one talks about this because banks and the über elite have been keeping it secret. Part of this is because artwork is correlated with the money supply. And our economy continues to print more and more money, expanding the coffers of the affluent. Guess who buys $10 million and $100 million pieces of art?

The holding period is anywhere between 3-10 years. That's the downside. But you know by the time an art piece is sold, it generates substantial profit (or it wouldn't be sold). And, without getting too morbid, when a current artist passes, their artwork value usually surges.

I'm currently about 3 years in on 150 pieces of art from 70 different artists. All of them are on track to perform in the 9-11% range, since it's a short term flip (for artwork anyhow).

All the artists I'm invested in have had public sales of their artwork in aggregate over $100M. So these aren't just some street fair artists making balloon animals. They come from in-demand names like Jeff Koons, who has sold over $750M of his art at public auctions. Actually, he *does* make balloon animals.

More alternative investing similar to this is on the horizon. You can already invest in the growth and output of farms at AcreTrader or FarmTogether; in the aging and eventual sale of vintage wines at VinoVest; or in cutting edge, scientific research at Experiment. I haven't determined how viable these are, or how one would make stable income with these. They may be too speculative for the banker's mindset. They are at least under my green banker's lamp for now.

If something can have value in the future, you can make money on it today. That's the prism for profit.

12

No-brainer Extra Income

"Try to save something while your salary is small;
it's impossible to save after you begin to earn more."

- Jack Benny

I eat out a lot, probably every day. I buy nice things. Quality is important to me. I live in a nice home. I frequently work from home, so my space is important.

I don't deprive myself of things. Life is too short to not explore, experience, and experiment. I design my life to be easy and enjoyable.

I have the privilege of all of this because I try to be mindful of the true costs of things. This takes deliberation. I can thoughtlessly go out, buy a bunch of stuff, and have a hangover later. That's easy. That's lazy. Anyone can do that. But it's not for me.

I prefer my freedom, which to me is the best definition of wealth. Because, after all, I've worked hard and made sacrifices to have this privilege in the first place. Why would I so easily give it away?

We can work hard and hike up that hill (desire/purpose) to fetch a bucket of water (goals/currency). But if the bucket has a hole in it (ignorance/noise), we reach the bottom of the hill with no water. So we repeat the process. Eventually, we end up like Jack and Jill.

This is the rat race most people sign-up for. Some don't realize it. They avoid the Now and live for the weekend. They play a round robin game of Who's On First thinking they're making progress. But they're just on a roundabout going nowhere. It feels like business, but it's busy-ness.

This is living pay-check to pay-check.

The Social Security Administration says over 50% of workers have to lean on friends and family at the end of their working life. They simply couldn't figure out in 40 years of working how to spend less than they make. Only 4% of all workers become stable (defined as having 6 months' emergency reserves), and only 1% are considered wealthy.

Almost 70% have less than $1,000 in savings. And of those, 50% have zero. That's a scary statistic. One medical bill, one layoff, one emergency away from potential homelessness.

"I love money. I love everything about it.
I bought some pretty good stuff. Got me a $300 pair of socks.
Got a fur sink. An electric dog polisher.
A gasoline powered turtleneck sweater.
And, of course, I bought some dumb stuff, too."

- Steve Martin

It's rarely about how much money you make, but rather how much you spend. It's a sad truism that broadcasting your commissions, bonuses, or increase in income brings more applause than do decreased debt and reduced expenses.

Can you imagine meeting someone at a party and asking, "So, how much debt do you carry for a living?"

People I know who make less than half what I do appear to make twice what I do. It's just an aggregate of choices. Optics have a heavy price.

If your expenses rise with your income, what's the point?

It's like the famous story of the Brazilian fisherman and the businessman (told in many languages and variations. I'm quoting from my own version in *Produce Yourself*):

A businessman is sitting on the beach in a beautiful Brazilian seaside town. He meets a local fisherman who is pulling up his little boat filled with large fish. Impressed, the businessman asks the fisherman how long it takes him to catch all these big fish. The fisherman replies that he does it in about 2 hours. Shocked, the businessman asked why he didn't simply stay out there longer and catch more. He could be rich.

The fisherman tells him that he doesn't need any more fish. This is more than enough to feed his whole family. And since it only takes him 2 hours, he's then able to return to his house, play with his kids, take a nap with his wife, join his buddies in the village for a drink, play guitar, sing and dance into the night.

The businessman can barely contain himself and explains how easily the fisherman could improve his process and be so much more effective. He should spend more time at sea, at least doubling or tripling his haul. Then he could buy a bigger boat, and then more boats, get crews of men, set up a cannery, have a whole distribution system of the best fresh Brazilian fish around. It would be so easy to upscale. He blows a huge opportunity by not realizing this.

The fisherman thinks about it for a few moments, then asks the businessman what it's all for. What's the purpose?

The businessman, frustrated by the fisherman's simple mind, tells him he could then retire rich. He could move somewhere by the ocean, buy a house, play with his kids, take a nap with his wife, join his buddies in the village for a drink, play guitar, sing and dance into the night. He wouldn't have to worry about money.

The fisherman asks the businessman, "Isn't that what I'm doing now?"

We think in terms of more. We're hard-wired to acquire and hoard as a means of survival and security, and also socially as an advertisement to others. This is who I am. I'm the kind of person who has X, wears Y, and drives Z.

We should be adopting a horizontal wealth strategy rather than a vertical one. The goal is keep expenses on a level plateau while increasing your income. If you increase your *earn*, don't also increase your *burn*. That just leaves you in ashes.

Thinking like a banker can (and will) add generous passive income to your portfolio. But it's all for naught if you don't turn off rising expenses as well.

"We buy things we don't need with money we don't have to impress people we don't like."

- Dave Ramsey

This is the cancer of our age.

Automating finances goes in both directions, so much so that we forget about things like monthly subscriptions and impulse purchases. They fly below the radar, undetected, until the bill comes. That bill becomes a credit card balance, which becomes debt, which becomes shackles, preventing the permissionless activities you seek by making more income.

Finances are the #1 reason couples get divorced. It's the #1 reason businesses fail. It's the #1 reason communities work or don't. No matter the organization, group, culture, whatever, it's finances.

We sometimes call it something else. We pinpoint other problems or personality. But when you step back, it's money. Money is the problem, or at least the instigator of the problem.

Steve Jobs died a Billionaire many times over at age 56. On his deathbed, he wrote:

"As we grow older, and hence wiser, we slowly realize that wearing a $300 or $30 watch - they both tell the same time...

Whether we carry a $300 or $30 wallet/handbag - the amount of money inside is the same;

Whether we drive a $150,000 car or a $30,000 car, the road and distance is the same, and we get to the same destination.

Whether we drink a bottle of $300 or $10 wine - the hangover is the same;

Whether the house we live in is 300 or 3000 sq ft - loneliness is the same.

You will realize your true inner happiness does not come from the material things of this world.

Whether you fly first or economy class, if the plane goes down - you go down with it..."

That last part reminds me of the Italian proverb, "At the end of the game, the king and the pawn go back in the same box." Sometimes a little perspective can help us with our finances.

Another billionaire is Amazon's Jeff Bezos. In 1999 he was featured on the TV show *60 Minutes*. He was only worth about $10 billion back then. The interview took place while Jeff drove the interviewer around in his car. When asked why he was driving an old Honda, Jeff laughed and said, "It's a perfectly good car."

Warren Buffett, Sam Walton - same thing. They have continued to preach that a lot of their wealth has come from knowing the difference between assets and liabilities. Things are liabilities. Assets are income streams. Buffett still lives in the same home he purchased for $30,000 in 1958. Walton, founder of Wal-Mart, drove the same 1979 Ford truck every day.

On the day Mark Zuckerberg married his college sweetheart, he was a billionaire. Yet he continued to drive a modest Acura, shop at The Gap, and host the wedding in their backyard.

For me, the point isn't to live miserly and be uncomfortable. It's that you think more clearly once you desire less stuff. The clearest thinkers have everything they want because stuff doesn't get in the way of more impactful pursuits. They have time to read, learn, be curious, ask questions, experiment, and make money. All of this happens when they spend less.

"Rich people have small TVs and big libraries,
and poor people have small libraries and big TVs."

- Zig Ziglar

Debt becomes a new story. We accept an unfulfilling job, a mediocre existence, and justify our unhappiness because we "have bills to pay." But that story merely outsources our own accountability. Somehow the narrative of having bills to pay is a communal theme. Everyone commiserates. There's social cohesion in this water-cooler complaint.

But having bills to pay is just a euphemism for an aggregate of past decisions we made to buy things. That's all. For some reason because credit cards bundle all of our specific debt decisions into one sum and call it a bill, it's now their fault, not ours.

The credit card company is cast as the villain. Yet if you purchase what you can afford, the credit card company loses. They make no money from you, the consumer. They only play the villain if you allow them to.

When the allure and dopamine of a purchase wears off, the hidden costs are painting, cleaning, accessorizing, fixing, protecting. This leads to contemplating, debating, thinking. Then maybe packing, moving, a wasted day with a yard sale, and eventually a trip to the storage unit where I make money from my syndicate.

Many of us can look at the items we bought over the last 12 months and discover that 20% of them are no longer in use. Some we wouldn't buy again were they to mysteriously vanish. This proves how much we enjoy the buying experience over the item itself. Neuroscientists will tell you that the dopamine hit comes from the actual buying, not the utility of the item.

"It is not the man who has too little,
but the man who craves more, that is poor."

All of the prior chapters' take-aways and tips are a complete waste of time, like the businessman's proposal to the fisherman, if you can't simultaneously plug the debt leaks. You will soon be making more money. You don't need to match those with more expenses. Otherwise, what's the point?

Here are my rules to patch those leaks so your bucket remains full:

1. The cost of anything is double what you pay.

I appropriately call this the double rule (I try to be creative with my titles). A $40,000 car truly costs $80,000 over its life, what with maintenance, repairs, insurance, taxes, leasing, and financing. The cost of a $750,000 house is $1.5 million (actually much more) over the life of the loan for similar reasons.

When you add ancillary and adjacent costs associated with stuff; and then factor in the amount of money you have to make *pre-tax* to equal that expense, it's often more than double. To afford the $10,000 camera, you have to make $14,000 before federal and state taxes. Now add in the lenses, the case, the straps, the mounts, etc. It's a $20k purchase minimum.

There's nothing wrong with quality assets. Buy that camera if it's an income stream or brings you joy beyond the first two weeks. Buy that camera if you are going on an amazing vacation and want to immortalize your photos. Just be cognizant of what you're buying, and acknowledge the undeniable long-term cost. That's the point.

2. Throw away double.

If you purchase an item, say a shirt, slacks, a new knick-knack for the office desk; then get rid of two. Coming home with a new pair of jeans? Donate two older pairs you know you'll never wear again, if you're honest with yourself. You hate how you look in them, but spent so much that day sauntering into that boutique with the perfect lighting and sounds of that song that inspires you, you can't part with them. Sunk cost. Get rid of them.

Create space in every sense of the word. Reduce decision fatigue. Increase willpower. Focus on what's important when your closet isn't a massive menu of options in which the server has to return 3 times because you still can't decide.

This allows you to make intentional purchases and minimize at the same time.

3. The 2-year rule.

You know what this is. What are you holding onto? It's been two entire cycles of holidays and you're not gonna wear that pumpkin sweater, use that fruit dehydrator, or break out the Gene Simmons edition of your broken air hockey table collecting dust.

4. Kill subscriptions.

Don't get rid of Netflix. Just be aware that the $15.99 a month you pay has cost you over $1,900 over the last 10 years you've used it.

Comb your statements and stop the $7 here and $12 there that occurs every month on those things you don't really use. Subscriptions are ingenious because $5 a month is nothing. But you wouldn't pay $180 a year so you can read that blog site the 6 times you visited over the last 3 years.

Want to make an extra 50 bucks a month in passive income? Reduce $35 a month in subscriptions and recurring charges somewhere for services you no longer use. Factoring in taxes, it's the same thing. You would have to make $50 before you're taxed to have $35 in available spending money to pay those $35 in expenses.

Here's some perspective. If you spend $27.40 a day for a year, that's $10,000 at the end of the year! We easily do that with a knick-knack here, a tchotchke there, or a souvenir of a windmill pencil sharpener because we can't travel home empty handed. We don't even own a pencil.

Why not eliminate the need for income you must make just to pay for the item you no longer care about anyway?

If you want to march up that hill and come back down with an empty bucket, so be it. But wouldn't you rather return from every journey with extra water to put into your well?

If I offered you the choice between $1 million dollars in cash today or a magical penny that would double in value every day for the next 30 days, which would you take?

For context, if you took the penny, on day 2 it would become 2 cents. On day 3 it would become 4 cents. On day 4, 8 cents and so on. After 10 of the 30 days, that penny would be worth $5.12.

This is why most respondents would take the $1 million cash.

But emphasizing the power of compound interest and long-term mindset, that penny is worth $10.7 million on day 30. And I don't have to tell you what that's worth if you wait one more day of doubling.

5. Learn

Before you become the bank to homebuyers, builders, and developers; before you lend to Wall Street and collect dividends; before you lend to people on P2P platforms; before you lend to Syndicates, DSTs, or to Bitcoiners, lend to yourself.

Time and time again, lending money to *you* before anyone or anything else has proven to be the most impressive thing you can do with your money. Yet many skip this modality because the results aren't immediately obvious.

I'm not talking about retirement. I think we all know it's better to stash money away for retirement than pay that same amount in taxes. It's a no-brainer to have and contribute regularly to IRAs, SEPs, 401ks. You're already on that.

I'm talking about self-education, learning, reading, and gaining a new skill. Take a new course. Satisfy curiosity. Earn a new license. Work to learn, not to earn; otherwise you're back on that treadmill.

"Any fool can know. The point is to understand."

- Albert Einstein

The money lent to yourself to digest these classes and hire these mentors will compound in ways you can't yet imagine. But opportunity and possibility is just on the other side of what you will learn, the contacts you will make, and the networks you will access.

College will help you find a career. But self-education will help you find wealth. You can't improve your finances if you don't improve your options.

Have a limitless and growth mindset. Welcome failure. Welcome obstacles. Welcome uncomfortable situations. There's an idea machine in all of us. But, like any muscle, it atrophies when we don't use it.

Come up with ideas every single day. Doesn't matter what it is, what it's for, or how unrealistic it is. Exercise that muscle. It's a gift that will keep on giving. Trust me on this one. Write it down. At the end of the year that's 365 ideas. Those ideas will spawn a new connection, new pursuit, or a breakthrough on a new approach.

Soon you'll see other mountains to climb and more buckets to carry. It's possible there's even a lake on the other side of that mountain. But how will you know if you don't make it to the other side?

More paramount than any of this is time.

We don't buy things with our coins and dollars. We buy it with our minutes and hours. When you frame your stuff in these terms, decisions are easier to make, that is, if you value your time.

So ask yourself, what's important to me? Protect your money. Protect your time. Plug the leaks. And plow ahead.

13

Bank Yourself For Infinite Value

"What we really want to do is what we are really meant to do.
When we do what we are meant to do, money comes to us,
doors open for us, we feel useful,
and the work we do feels like play to us."

- Julia Cameron

In this last chapter, I focus on the least passive financial strategies. They are perhaps the most compelling, as they involve who you are and what you do.

You have a special set of skills, experience, and background. You are unique in that way.

Sometimes imposter syndrome runs deep. But the truth is, anyone can do whatever they want to occupy their time. The difference between what you do and what someone else does is merely a sequence of deliberate and prioritized steps.

Those steps most likely weren't a direct ascension, even if you went to automotive school and became a mechanic. You likely have a particular blend of personal taste, acquired hobbies, and specialized talents that intersect in a place of ideas and opportunity.

Proximity Potential is a term I coined in *Produce Yourself*. We sit in a space close to our interests and hobbies that others can't access. Our lives make up a signature Venn-diagram where professional networks, geography, academic background, inherent nature, and passions live. New configurations are formed as curiosity leads you down new paths.

This makes us valuable to someone, beyond personal or emotional connection. It's how we get hired. It's why we can negotiate salary or fees. Because we're not robots, we bring that blend of human ingredients to the chef's table.

So we lend out the most valuable asset we have. We lend who we are to others.

This is the ultimate and most exclusive form of "private banking," since no one else can lend you but you. Unfortunately, some people don't solve a rare enough problem or do it in a way that others find useful.

People complain about their salary or fees, yet don't self-reflect on that thing they do. They want to charge more when their focus should be on being better and providing more. These same complainers are the ones who fill an interchangeable and mechanical role. They cast blame on the system, on the corporation, on "the man."

Every product or service that you've ever used or heard of is based on one simple idea: help people get what they want. By helping others get what they want, the entrepreneur gets what she wants. It's a never ending cycle of problem-solution; problem-solution. That's business school, condensed.

So we lend our ability to problem solve. We rent out our time for 40, 50, or maybe even 100 hours a week to a company. During this time period, they own us. This is why employers want exclusivity. It's why they monitor us. It's why we sign NDAs.

The hours we're on the clock, however, are mostly a waste of time. When you subtract meaningless meetings, wasted interruptions, distractions, coffee breaks, conference calls, lunches, email chains, and the seemingly ceaseless politics of titles and office size, your effectual output is roughly 2-3 hours. The rest is wasted to the corporate dance (or boxing).

2-3 hours of focused, deep work will beat 10 hours of open-space distractions, interruptions, and multitasking. When you protect your time at work, you can use the typically wasted hours more effectively. This is money in the bank. Your bank.

Unless you hate your job, don't leave it. Passion and purpose *follow* skills, not the other way around. But we misinterpret a bad work environment, a toxic leader, or a broken corporate culture. We may think we hate what we do. Often it's not what we do but whom we do it for.

You have the right to refuse service to anyone. Stop lending out all your time to a bad customer. You not only lend yourself to the wrong people, you neglect your best customer: yourself. That's the customer you care about.

Don't waste those idle hours just to fill space so you can look at the clock to see when it's okay to sneak out to drive home to then check emails to see what unimportant task has been labeled as urgent by your coworkers.

Protect your time. Say "No." "No" is the most effective and efficient productivity tool ever (the 2nd most effective is turning off WiFi). Focus on your work. And then focus on lending your work to customers other than the one to whom you just gave your whole day.

We love to hear stories about people who quit their jobs and become overnight successes with their idea. But here's the truth: they started that process years before they left their job. It wasn't overnight. They leveraged the infrastructure, contacts, and reach of their current employment. They spent time learning, researching, building, and putting together the foundation for something new. It provided them the opportunity to lend themselves on the side.

This is where opportunity begins for the *active* banker's life. It's not passive. It's not automatic. But it's where you can turn your *Why* into lending rates that will magnify 100-fold.

Slide down the corporate ladder and you'll find someone just starting out. You may be 10, 20, or 30 years into your career. Your proximity potential is valuable to the person just starting theirs today. They can accelerate their day 1 into maybe month 9 or year 3, all because of you.

People might kill to be able to tap your brain and ask questions. People may pay to rent your knowledge, advice, and help.

Imagine yourself at age 20. What would it be worth to have a conversation with whom you are now? Could you not have saved yourself a ton of money and time?

It's easy to think, "Why me?" You know what you know so it doesn't seem so special to you. That's the Curse of Knowledge, a cognitive bias that assumes since you know something, others must as well. You live it every day. But you forget where you were when you wanted to be where you are today.

You would have given anything to participate in some of the pursuits you currently enjoy. But the seasoned version of you forgets this. The girl or boy in us has stopped dreaming of adventure because the reality of bosses and an office ecosystem has taken the wind out of our sails. We are sold adulthood as compliance and approval.

Maybe after you make some money and gain more accolades, you'll be ready. Maybe someday in the future you can think about monetizing who you are. But someday never comes. Tomorrow is where dreams go to die.

I fall prey to this Curse of Knowledge. I forget that others haven't sold TV shows; raised financing for movies; *made* movies and TV shows; leveraged real estate financing; rehabbed houses; started companies; sold companies; and haven't taken the time to think about their process and approach to what it is they do all day and *why* they do it.

This knowledge ping pongs around in my head all day that I just assume it isn't special, it isn't valuable. It's just a collection of items I've picked up here and there on my journey. But like you, like everyone, I have a modicum of knowledge that may help others.

I implore you to go help someone. Lend out YOU. And, in the process, you will help yourself.

"We make a living by what we get,
but we make a life by what we give."

Self-education is the fastest growing industry in the world right now. The pandemic of Covid-19 has only cemented this. People want access and acceleration. They want a course, a webinar, a video series. They want one-on-one consulting, Zoom seminars, Gumroad classes, text lessons (check out Arist.com). They want to read a book, blog, or series of social posts from someone who can share their advice and tips.

"You can have everything you want in life if you will just help other people get what they want."

•Zig Ziglar

Need to kill time at work to fill space? Kill it with a process or system where you rent out your idle knowledge, experience, access, wisdom, and stories to others.

Is there *one* person who would benefit from listening to you for an hour of undivided attention to lay it all out for them? I bet there is one person who cherishes your advice. If you have an audience of one, you can build a tribe. One becomes 10, and 10 becomes 100. And so on.

This is the curation of tomorrow. Gone are the days where you need to appeal to the masses. If you can solve a problem for one person, the vaccine will spread. The new economy we are experiencing is all about niche silos. Finding and exploiting the nooks and crannies of specificity open the gates for new floods of income.

You have a phone. You have a computer with a camera. You have Internet access. You can type. You can talk. You can write. And you have YOU. You don't need anything more than YOU.

Realize that you have resources in your head not earning interest. They are in a savings account at .01% - safe and insured, but decreasing in value with time.

Sadly, most people are more concerned with looking stupid than making money. They are governed by living up to the opinions of others. That's the biggest difference between whom we want to be, and whom we are.

Remain hidden. Don't make a fool of yourself. Don't be unsophisticated. Sit in the dugout, and you'll never swing and miss.

But what's the price of that?

If I write something, people will read it. If I make a video, people will see it. If I broadcast a podcast people will hear my lame jokes. If my name is on a movie or TV show, it's on me. But I show up. I march on.

It turns out quantity precedes quality. If you don't believe me, look back at the first iterations of any product, service, or brand you consume.

What happens if people laugh at this little book? What happens if people see a post I made on Instagram and don't like it? What happens if others don't agree with my opinions or my art.

I already know the answer if I don't show up. I already know the answer if I don't publish, telecast, or submit. You have to ship it. You have to send it out into the world.

If I'm not perhaps cringing years later, then I'm not growing. But that's how evolution works. Seed to tree. Tree to orchard. Orchard to abundance.

Here's the revelation: we put out our best work the day we stop caring how other people will judge us.

A study was conducted wherein a ceramics professor divided his art class on day 1 into two groups. Group A was tasked with creating one perfect pot. They would be judged entirely on quality. Group B was tasked with making as many pots as possible. They would be graded solely on quantity.

At the end of the semester a peculiarity surfaced: Group B, who simply had to make as many pots as they could, ended up making the highest quality pots. While Group B was churning out pot after pot, they learned and perfected their process. They perfected their skills from repetition.

Group A sat theorizing and analyzing so much on how to make the highest quality pot that their ideas failed to translate, due to procrastination and inexperience.

We always hear how everything is about quality, not quantity. But you need quantity to discover quality in the first place. Otherwise, you're paralyzed waiting for that perfect moment to make that perfect thing. And perfection is a debilitating concept that doesn't really exist.

I have a one-on-one consulting business that was born from *Produce Yourself*. Now I rent out portions of my time. And my time is valuable. I charge accordingly.

Consulting and strategizing for others grew from areas of my life I was passionate about. It wasn't easy accepting my first client. Who am I? I've never done this. How can I provide value? However, that was just a story I told myself to stay safe and comfortable. But quantity eventually helped get me to quality.

And, of interest, my first clients were in the same boat. They had knowledge, skills, and great connections and never thought about that being special to someone else. But now they've written books, started businesses, and are consultants in their own right.

I've discovered that by chipping away, compounding efforts, little by little, just 1% a day, I have quietly automated income to the point I have more and more permissionless activities in my life. And I think true happiness dwells in the permissionless life.

If something excites me and I know it will be an incredible experience learning something new, and working with creative people, then I engage. I crave these collaborations and projects. They feed me. But if not, I'm happy to pass. People don't have to know why. They don't have to know the superpower that exists in thinking like a banker.

The pillars of ultimate wealth creation are:

- Learning from your mistakes (chapter 2)

- Collecting on loans (chapters 3 and 7)

- Adapting to the future (chapters 4 and 5)

- Buying equities (chapter 6)

- Investing in real estate (chapters 8-10)

- Monetizing the value of time (chapter 11)

- Harnessing expenses (chapter 12)

- And most crucially, leveraging yourself (this chapter)

So what are you waiting for? What's holding you back? Who cares what anyone thinks? Bankers don't care that you laugh at them. They're laughing all the way to the bank.

At some point, you must make your income independent of your time, if you want to have time for others.

Live the Banker's life. It's a privilege everyone should enjoy.

Please join me on Instagram @ProduceYourself. I'd love to hear from and learn more about you.

You can also find me at TerenceMichael.com where I offer tailored consulting and financial strategy.

Now go out there and *Make Bank*.

www.ingramcontent.com/pod-product-compliance
Lightning Source LLC
Chambersburg PA
CBHW081819200326

41597CB00023B/4315